C000301385

Everyday Miracles

Everyday Miracles

True Stories That Could Change Your Life

Jonathan Collins

© Vega 2002

Text © Jonathan Collins 2002

All rights reserved. No part of this book may be reproduced,
stored in a retrieval system or transmitted in any form
or by any means, electronic, mechanical, photocopying,
recording or otherwise, without the prior permission
in writing of the copyright owners.

ISBN 1-84333-022-9

A catalogue record for this book is available from the British Library

First published in 2002 by

Vega
64 Brewery Road
London, N7 9NT

A member of the Chrysalis Group plc

Visit our website at www.chrysalisbooks.co.uk
Printed in Great Britain by Creative Print and Design (Wales)

CONTENTS

Author's Preface   *ix*

1. The Unobstructed Path   1
   Trust

2. Rescue Juice   9
   Healing

3. Jay's Sign   21
   Patience

4. Shattered in the Canyon   37
   Serenity

5. Harp Magic   51
   Harmony

6. Transforming Grief to the Eleventh Power   65
   Creativity

7. A Marvelous Game   85
   Strength

8. Death of a Husband   95
   Courage

9. Death of a Wife   121
    Acceptance

10. Death of a Son   133
    Non-Attachment

11. Moment of Recognition   145
    Intimacy

12. Communion with Darkness   161
    Unanimity

13. The Wish-fulfilling Tree   171
    Gratitude

14. The Way Home   187
    Grace

15. Blessings in the Vegetable Garden   197
    Life

16. Enter the Spa Goddess   207
    Order

17. A Symphony of Healing   219
    Love

Dedicated to Angeline, Alexi and Emily,
my three pearls beyond price.

AUTHOR'S PREFACE

"There are only two ways to live your life. One is as though nothing is a miracle. The other is as though everything is a miracle."

Albert Einstein

Everything under the sun, and all that lies beyond it, is a miracle. If we cleanse our inner eye, it is possible to see this and to live in a state of continuous wonder. Our perception of life is then transformed: where there was randomness, now there is a mysterious order to things, and every event becomes precious and meaningful.

Of course, it is easy to experience this perspective when life is going well; it's much harder when we're in the middle of crisis and suffering. That's why many of the seventeen stories in this book portray people who have experienced severe challenges. I found myself drawn to individuals who could look me in the eye and, with complete authenticity, say, "Even then, in the

ix

bleakest of times, Life had a gift for me, and here's what that gift was."

This is the secret to living a life filled with miracles —namely, seeing the opportunity that is contained in every situation. Then our spiritual growth accelerates beyond our wildest dreams, and joy and certainty become constant features of our inner landscape.

For the most part, the people appearing in *Everyday Miracles* live in Ojai, a picturesque town in Southern California. Consequently, their experiences, and the way they interpret them, tend to have a Californian flavor. However, we are all part of a collective consciousness—a shared wisdom—and so I hope that the quest for spiritual understanding portrayed in this book will succeed in transcending cultural differences.

I believe that everything in your life is miraculously orchestrated, including the fact that you are reading these words right now. It is my sincere wish that the stories and spiritual insights contained in these pages fulfill their mission and encourage you on your journey into the Light.

Jonathan Collins
Ojai, California

"Those who trust us educate us."

Proverb

THE UNOBSTRUCTED PATH
Trust

I have been thinking about writing "Everyday Miracles" for some time, but procrastination and inertia have been obstructing the project. Then Life gives me a nudge. In a pivotal conversation with the woman who inspired this book, I learn something about the miracle of trust.

IT IS 6:00 A.M. and the Southern California town of Ojai is slowly waking up. I have just removed a bundle of unexciting mail from my post office box and am intending to return home. Life, however, has other plans for me.

I breathe deeply, filling my lungs with the invigorating morning air. Although it is nearly spring, there is still a dusting of snow on Chief Peak, Topa Topa and on several other mountains surrounding the valley. The temperature dropped below freezing during the night and giant silver propellers on white towers roared above the orange groves, mixing up the layers of warm and cold air so the trees wouldn't freeze.

Now the sun is creeping over the eastern hills, each ray momentarily distinct from every other, and the valley is already warming up. The air is filled with the smell of sage, eucalyptus and citrus fruits. Woodpeckers busily hammer at the trunks of dwarf oak trees and shimmering hummingbirds dart about in search of pink blossoms.

A beam of golden sunlight falls on Ojai's Spanish-style downtown. The buildings are white stucco with tile roofs. At the west end of the town, where I am standing, a bell in the post office tower loudly chimes the hour. At the east end, a huge cloud of aromatic smoke billows out of the Ojai Coffee Roasting Company: the day's beans are being roasted. If you live within half a mile of downtown, you have no option but to wake up and smell the coffee.

The aroma is as enticing as a siren's song, but I have work to do. I start to get into my car. And then I hear the "Voice." It is an infrequent visitor to my inner world, but a distinct one. It generally gives an instruction or a piece of advice, and it does so in a quiet way, even if the message is urgent. Once it saved me from serious injury on a treacherous road in Provence; on another occasion it found me exactly the right job in Santa Barbara; and recently it directed me to a wonderful partner, whom I might otherwise easily have spent a lifetime ignoring. Today, it appears to be delving into the mundane, for it has softly suggested that I do go to the coffeehouse. I present it with compelling arguments against the plan. It gently repeats its suggestion. I obey. I'm learning to trust it.

The coffeehouse is owned by Kent and Stacey. Kent is fascinated by the art of roasting and brewing exquisite coffee, and he excels at the task. Stacey is the perfect hostess, with a rare talent for making every customer feel welcome and special. Marty and Jeff serve the coffee. Gifted musicians at night, by day they bring artistry to the job of making espresso.

The place is genuine and many Ojai residents sense it. Actors, musicians, teachers, business people, writers, film-makers, massage therapists, landscape gardeners, bankers, wine-makers, acupuncturists and artists all patronize the establishment and fill it with the sound of chinking cups, laughter and the buzz of animated conversation.

I enter the coffeehouse and am surprised to spot Leslie Merical sitting at a hand-painted table in the corner. She is eating a bagel and sipping a cappuccino. She's a friend I've known for years, but she lives on the coast, fifteen miles away, and so her visits to Ojai are rare, especially at this hour of the morning.

The sight of her jogs my memory. I feel ashamed. I realize that I have done nothing about a project we discussed last time we met, which was for me to write a book called *Everyday Miracles*. I wonder whether the "Voice" has directed me here in order to rekindle my resolve.

I sit down at Leslie's table and Marty brings me a coffee. They are both excited because their band, Left of Memphis, has just completed its first CD, and they're proud of it. A shipment of CDs arrived at Leslie's house last night and she couldn't wait to bring a copy up here. "This is it playing now," she informs me.

The music is beautiful and the lyrics reach into deep places. The CD is touched with magic, and I tell them so.

Leslie thanks me for the compliment and then leans across the table purposefully. I can tell her mind has turned to a subject I would rather avoid—*Everyday Miracles.* "Have you started it yet?" she inquires. I confess that I haven't.

Leslie is a wise woman. She sees instantly the essence of a situation and communicates it resolutely. I watch her eyes: there's a liveliness in them; I can tell she's about to delve into my psyche and give my soul a compassionate shake.

"Lack of self-trust is what holds us back," she begins, in a gentle tone. "It operates at a deep level of principle, causing us to do things—like procrastinate or be needy or pessimistic—that we wouldn't normally allow ourselves to do. It makes us create obstacles and confusions that don't really exist. When we trust ourselves, we are empowered to act according to our own nature and our deepest truth.

"Lack of self-trust can be healed by taking action —action we are able to successfully complete, so that we may feel the satisfaction of accomplishment. It's an exercise for the psyche. As with physical exercise, we start with something small and then progressively stretch ourselves. As we do so, we build up deposits in our self-trust account.

"Your first step for self-trust, Jonathan, is to complete the book. It's been touched by something very good. It will allow other people some insight into you, and it will give you something to live up to.

"In my experience, every one of us has a unique path with no obstructions. First we have to see the path, and this involves contacting our deepest and purest feelings about what we are supposed to do with our lives. Secondly, we need to overcome our inertia and take action. Thirdly, we have to change our perception about what we experience—we no longer see obstacles, we only see signposts helping us along our way. As we develop self-trust, and align ourselves with our deepest passion, we understand that obstacles and confusions are all illusory. We begin to see a clear, unobstructed path stretching before us.

"A searchlight is focused on your path, Jonathan, and only blindness could prevent you from seeing it. It's so clear—your talent is spilling from you all over the place. You've been given a gift, and the path that is so clearly laid out for you is to use it.

"You've been destined to make an impact as a writer for as long as I've known you. I remember clearly the first day I met you and my impression: I had the feeling that I was in the presence of someone with the potential to do great good. A lot of people feel that way about you.

"Write this book. Go to the right place and trust that your life will be better for it. Don't assume that financial success is the best reward you can receive. You don't want to second-guess serendipity. It does have a special gift to offer you, and you as a humble human being will be able to receive it and appreciate its beauty.

"Allow the message that is coming to you, asking for expression, to reveal itself. That's enough, and it's something you need to trust. Feel when you're going in other directions, and stop it. You don't need those other directions any more. They haven't taken you where you want to go.

"Write the book, Jonathan. Your moment is here. Trust it. It's real."

The Miracle of Trust is that it reveals to us the perfection of every instant of existence. The self-trust that Leslie advocated is, at its most extreme, complete faith in the flawlessness of the universe.

Trust invites us to experiment with a new approach to living. It asks us to consider that our conditioned view of life, absorbed by osmosis from society, is based on the illusion that we are separate from a world which, unless we take action, will harm us.

Life asks us to experience every event without judgment or expectation. Into the deepest recesses of our heart, it whispers a promise to us: "Trust the moment, without knowing why, and you will discover a priceless gift, the fruit of an inconceivable love."

The gift is seldom what we anticipate, but it is always what we need. As we increasingly trust this process, energies are released that carry us to the farthest reaches of our talents and potential, to places beyond our wildest dreams.

7

"There is no curing a sick man who believes himself in health."

Henri Amiel

RESCUE JUICE
Healing

Megan recalls her teenage years, when she was diagnosed with leukemia. In order to survive, she had to regain something she'd lost many years before the illness—her will to live. As she struggled to save her life, she realized she was being given an opportunity to heal on a deeper level than just the physical body. This is the miracle of healing.

MEGAN IS PERCHED expectantly on the edge of a chair, waiting for my first question. She has the vitality, and much of the innocence, of a young child. She radiates a clear energy that would make you trust her completely about anything.

We are sitting outside Rescue Juice, a bright red fire truck that has been converted by Megan and her husband into a mobile coffee and juice bar. It is a fabulous contraption, with a touch of genius in it. I hired them recently to do the catering for a one-day

Deepak Chopra seminar, and their truck was universally appreciated—a little gem dispensing delicious fresh drinks and snacks, and good will.

Megan's skin is pale, but clear and healthy. Her eyes are lustrous. It is only under the eyes that there's a telltale sign of what she's been through: a darkness that suggests residues of toxicity.

She first became sick fourteen years ago, when she was seventeen. She'd been hanging out with a fast crowd—running around, staying out late and disobeying her parents. Her extreme paleness and constant tiredness were attributed to physical overload, until finally her mother insisted on taking her for a blood test.

It was a Friday night when she went to the hospital to hear the results. She was feeling impatient because her friends were expecting to take her to a party and she wasn't sure they would wait for her. Her major concern was what to wear that night and if there'd be enough tequila to go around.

Then the doctor spoke, and everything her life had been up to that point vanished into thin air. There would be no more parties; no more lover's tiffs with her boyfriend; no more margaritas; no more weekend jaunts to Palm Springs with her girlfriends. She had leukemia, and the news was so huge and indigestible that her mind froze and she went into shock. Then, slowly, the full significance of the diagnosis dawned on her: every single second of her day, every last cell in her body, every drop of energy she could muster, every part of her, at all times, was going to be mobilized in the fight to save her life.

And as she reflected on this, she saw something miraculous. For years she had been suicidal; she couldn't deal with feelings and she couldn't deal with people; all her partying and wildness had been an attempt to run away from the pain. Now, in this moment of disaster, she saw that her death wish was not a real part of her nature. As she sat there listening to the doctor's litany of warnings—the treatment would be long, painful and debilitating; she would lose all her hair; her immune system would be devastated and she might contract any one of an array of serious diseases; after going through hell, she might still die—she realized that, in the core of her being, she had an irrepressible will to survive. In the midst of her terror, she experienced a strange sense of elation.

"I spent a month in the hospital," she tells me, "and then I went through nearly two years of chemotherapy. On one occasion I fell into a coma for a week. I had a reaction to a chemotherapy medication, which knocked my white cell count down to zero, and then I contracted viral encephalitis. Whether it was from a mosquito or

11

what they don't know—there had been a lot of mosquitoes around that summer. I just went crazy, delirious—talking to people who weren't there, unable to recognize people who were there. One night, I went into seizures and the hospital called my parents in because it looked like I wasn't going to make it, or, if I survived, that I'd be brain-damaged. But I pulled through.

"Finally, I went into remission and spent a year or two 'somewhat well.' Although the illness had given me a warning, I guess the lesson didn't really take root in me: I went back to drinking and partying until, one day, I realized that I was sick again. There were telltale signs, such as bruising and bleeding gums, but basically I just knew intuitively that it had returned.

"When my self-diagnosis was confirmed, I was even more terrified than the first time. I knew that chemotherapy was not an option the second time around and that my chances of survival had plummeted dramatically.

"I was admitted to the hospital for a bone marrow transplant. They radiated my body for six hours—the equivalent of 62,000 chest x-rays—in order to kill the bone marrow, and then they performed the transfusion from my sister.

"There were moments when I prayed to die, because the pain and the fatigue of the radiation were so intense; however, deep down I knew I was not the person I had been before—now I was someone who truly wanted to be alive. A lot of perks go with being sick, and I saw that no part of me wanted them anymore. I got rid of every part of me that was fascinated with death. I was simply determined to live. I used to have to cheer up my family. I'd make a video for them and say, 'I'm OK and I'm going to survive this next treatment.'

"I remember my doctors had this spiel each time to protect themselves from a malpractice suit: 'We're going to give you this much chemotherapy, and the result could be death; we're going to give you this much radiation, and the result could be death.' Then they wanted my signature agreeing to the treatments. I made an arrangement with them—they would read the text while I plugged my ears, and then I'd sign the paper without looking at it. I didn't want to hear or think anything negative.

"After two months of treatment, I was told that it was over. I had recovered. The physicians said all I needed now was to go home and convalesce. 'Go home?' I thought. 'They do all this stuff to you for the longest time, and then they just say go home and get better?'

"After the treatments I had this baby immune system. I couldn't breathe the air (I had to wear a

13

mask), I couldn't speak to people, and I couldn't eat anything that might have the slightest virus in it, not even yogurt. I had no hair and I was emaciated. My grandmother said I looked like I'd just been freed from Auschwitz. It was pathetic; I'd walk two steps and be exhausted. I couldn't take a bath. I felt like this little, vulnerable freak.

"The convalescence was a long, hard road. It took me another five years to regain sufficient strength to work full time. Nevertheless, I don't ever regret having been sick. Every moment of my life is precious now, and I am in awe of it as I watch it unfold so beautifully.

"The highlight has been marrying my husband, Tom. He was living on a boat in the Channel Islands harbor when I met him; we started seeing each other and five months later we were married.

"That was three years ago. So far it's been fabulous and, at the same time, immensely challenging. I feel confident in the relationship, but that's not because of an absence of challenges; it's more that I have a deep conviction that I know how to deal with anything that comes up. When an issue arises, instead of needing to run away, as I did in the past, I welcome it. 'What little pearl,' I wonder, 'is going to come out of this one?' I don't always feel that way in the heat of the moment, but the gap is getting smaller all the time.

"For our honeymoon we went on a six-week trip, driving across the country to Nova Scotia. I have no idea why we chose Nova Scotia of all places.

"In any case, a wonderful synchronicity took place. We had been talking about starting a mobile juice bar when Tom and I returned to California. On our trip, in upstate New York, we visited Tom's stepfather, who was a volunteer firefighter, and his fire station had this old fire truck. Tom showed it to me excitedly and said how great it would be as a juice bar. It was kind of this big old thing, and I jokingly said, 'What are you going to call it—Rescue Juice?'

"We asked to buy it and at first they refused. We continued on to Canada and throughout the trip we kept running into fireman things. In Nova Scotia, for example, we got stuck in the mud at low tide. When the car was finally towed out, it was filthy, and somebody suggested that we go and clean it at a fire station in the next village. The fireman there was all excited to have visitors from California. He dressed us up in firefighter uniforms and we washed the truck with a fire hose.

"That evening, on our voice mail, we received a message that the fire station did want to sell the truck after all. So, on our way back from Nova Scotia, we went by the station, hooked our car to the back of the fire truck and drove it—shaking, rattling and

15

humming—all the way across the country to California. We sold everything—the Scout (Tom's baby that he'd built) and a couple of boats, one of which we'd been living on—and with the proceeds we converted the truck into Rescue Juice."

"There's something that puzzles me about that," I say to Megan. "In addition to health-giving juices, you sell every form of coffee. Coffee's an addictive drug, and I wonder how you feel about selling a product that's toxic, something you wouldn't want to take yourself."

"I think the problem with coffee is more with the pesticides than the caffeine itself, and so many of our coffees are organic. Moreover, a lot of people go to coffeehouses for something other than the coffee —not just for other drinks, like juices or teas, but for the atmosphere and society. When I'm at the hospital working the coffee cart, I deal all day long with sick people who are scared and lonely. I see them brighten up and come alive around the cart, and I think how much more healing it is than detrimental.

"Although caffeine may over-stimulate you, and coffee acids can be bad for the stomach, at least you're not going to get high and go out and rob or kill somebody. So I think it's an evolution of consciousness that coffeehouses are growing in popularity and bars are becoming less prevalent. Many coffee shops already sell fresh juices, and in the future I think a lot of them will add a complete juice menu, as we have done.

"And coffee is something of an art form. There are different beans, countries, altitudes, forms of roasting, etc—it's got a nobility to it, like wine. If you couldn't have an espresso served to you at Rescue Juice, it would all be kind of dull, a little too serious."

Megan glances back at the Rescue Juice fire truck, and I can tell she's itching to get back there and push carrots, celery and apples through her industrial-strength juicer. But there's one more thing I want to know. I ask her if there is anything she's afraid of now that she's stared death in the face and seen that it was her friend, not her enemy.

She thinks for a moment and then says quietly: "The other day, I was listening to a Carolyn Myss tape and it scared me. It brought up the fear that Tom or I would eventually grow away from our relationship, that the universe would separate us. I felt terrible, but then I thought about it deeply and I realized I'd be OK. Every so-called catastrophic experience contains something very precious. Beforehand, we can't imagine what that might be. We have to live the experience with an open heart and mind, and then we find the gift. This is what I learned from my illness, and I trust it.

17

"I don't feel that the universe victimizes us. Somehow we invite our own lessons. This doesn't mean we're good or bad—it's somewhere outside of good and bad. There's an intelligence at work and, however hard our path might seem, it is working for our benefit."

The Miracle of Healing is that it helps us remember our true nature and regain our original wholeness. As Megan discovered, physical illness is an outer manifestation of this deeper imperative.

We are separated from our essence by wounds received early in life, and perhaps in past lives too. These wounds are like black holes guarded by terrible dragons. The dragons are our fears. If we confront them, they can be seen for what they are—illusions— and they disappear. The black holes are then filled with our essence, and our communion with the source of authentic love, strength, compassion and every other virtue is renewed. Life's purpose is to guide us into making this reconnection with our fundamental nature.

During this process of healing, a beautiful surprise is revealed to us—in reality, there is nothing that needs to be healed. It is all a case of mistaken identity. The body/mind we inhabit is not the ultimate truth of who we are. At our core we are something unimaginably vast, something absolutely vital that can never be harmed.

Because of impatience we were driven out of Paradise, because of impatience we cannot return.

W.H. Auden

JAY'S SIGN
Patience

A new life begins for Jay, brought to him in an intriguing display of dreams and synchronicities. He discovers the miracle of patience: when we let go and wait, everything is ultimately given to us.

HE HAS A MASTER'S in psychology from Harvard and a degree in philosophy and literature from the Sorbonne. His name is Jay. He is forty-five and claims his mid-life crisis started twenty years ago. Occasionally, he says, light appears at the end of the tunnel; but so far it has always proved to be an illusion.

His fortieth birthday seemed particularly auspicious, he tells me. He spent it at the Ojai Foundation, a retreat center located on a beautiful hill at the heart of Ojai's power spot. Its gardens are a spectacular interplay of nature and art. Teepees and yurts are dotted around the property, and a huge circular meditation deck overhangs a ravine. There is a kiva and a sweat lodge. A giant, whitewashed Buddha surveys the scene from atop an altar, and appears satisfied.

Evening came and the sun began to set at the far end of the valley. Behind him a full moon rose. The sun and the moon and his head lay in a straight line. It was surely an omen. He was elated. Stripped down to his essence, he was now confident that he could rebuild his life on a sound foundation. The inner voice told him that his protracted phase of quiet desperation was over. It was time to shake off the past and step into the destiny that was awaiting him.

Within three years, he had lost his business, his money, his wife (divorce) and his father (cancer). He was unemployed, heartbroken and drunk. Worse still, he felt unemployable and too drained to build up another business from scratch.

Listening to him recount his woes to me, I am reminded of Eeyore, the depressed donkey in *Winnie-the-Pooh.* I tell him this, and he laughs.

"It's the worst of times and the best of times," he says. "I rise every morning at 3:00 A.M. and drive to the Von's supermarket parking lot in a barely serviceable car bought by a friend who has never been repaid. There I fold three hundred *Ventura County Star* newspapers, my fingers stiff from the cold, and cracked and bleeding from the absorbent action of the paper. Having piled the papers into the car—they fill every available cubic inch, and much of the driving area too—I cruise around town and throw them on to porches and driveways. I return home at 6:00 A.M., often completely drenched by torrential rains. I sleep only a few hours a night, and I'm so tired I'm numb.

"But it is wonderful too. In my expanded moments, Sufi like, I see it all as just another experience. Viewed as a movie, it's quite an entertaining experience at that. We are a motley group that gathers in the parking lot at 3:00 A.M. There's a woman who was an English professor until she lost her memory as a result of a car crash. She's been delivering papers for twelve years now. Her hands are arthritic and she can't grasp or lift the bundles of newspapers as they are unloaded from the truck. Her colleagues help her. She spends her days reading four or five potboiler novels every day. She's lost her taste for the classics, but not her enjoyment of reading.

"The supervisor in the parking lot is a woman with a four-year-old son. Simply put, she's a really decent person. So-called illumined beings could take her correspondence course. She works all night from eleven to seven, and then spends the day looking after her son. She has to work, but she refuses to have the child raised in daycare. She didn't give birth to him never to see him. Asked when she sleeps, she replies: 'Rarely.' Sleep is a luxury she can't afford.

"They are beautiful people out there in that miserably cold parking lot. Really beautiful. They'd do anything for you. Who's to say I'm worse off than in the Texaco boardroom? Can you imagine what that would be like?

"Nevertheless, it appears that the tide is turning for me. A lovely woman called Anne has recently come into my life in a miraculous way. I was guided to her by dreams and synchronicities, as if the whole universe had turned its hand to matchmaking. It makes me hopeful that I'm at a turning point because I've noticed that, just as everything seems to collapse at the same time in a person's life—career, relationship, finances, even health—so does every aspect of one's life begin to blossom at the same time. That's my experience anyway and it's why I view her miraculous presence in my life as a good omen.

"I first met Anne at the house of an acquaintance. After meeting me in a restaurant for a business dinner, he invited me home to look at his Website. She wandered into the living room and was introduced to me as his housemate. As with any female between the age of fifteen and fifty-five, my relationship radar scanner became fully operational: I pegged her as being one of those overbearing women who would drive you nuts within a few days. She was wearing a white terry-cloth bathrobe that had seen better days and I think she was wearing glasses too. After a few minutes, she wandered back to her bedroom, saying that she had to 'feng shui' her room—Anne-speak for 'pick up a few books and put my undies in the laundry hamper.' Beyond that, I didn't give her another thought.

"That night, however, I had a vivid dream that seemed to last for hours. There were a dozen different scenes, in each of which I was looking for a woman. I could see her features, but not distinctly enough to make out who she was, and I didn't know her name or where she lived. In one scene I was sitting at a picnic table in some woods outside a log cabin, when she appeared briefly and then left. I realized that I still didn't know who she was and that I kept missing the opportunity to find out.

"At the end of the dream, when it appeared likely that the woman would remain forever anonymous, a clear voice, seemingly from outside me, said: 'The woman you are looking for is called Anne.'

"I awoke puzzled. Even though I had just met Anne the day before, she didn't come to mind in connection with the dream. I couldn't think of any Anne I knew whom I would be 'looking for.'

"That afternoon, I was in Rainbow Bridge, the health food store, paying for some snacks, when a woman,

25

seated at a table in the restaurant area, waved at me. I vaguely recognized her, but I couldn't quite make out her features. I whispered to the clerk, 'It's embarrassing when somebody knows you and you don't have a clue who they are.' At that instant, I suddenly realized I was reliving a scene in my dream. Just as in the dream, all I could make out was thick, long, sandy-colored hair. As in the dream, I was peering at a woman unable to place her or remember her name. I realized, still unable to see her features, that the woman greeting me was Anne.

"As I approached her, I saw that without the bathrobe and glasses she was a beautiful woman. I sat down briefly at her table, where she was eating fried tofu and drinking fresh carrot juice, and we chatted politely. Still, the relationship/friendship scanner wasn't beeping, and so I left after a few minutes without thinking anything more about it.

"That night, I dreamt of her again. We were sitting in a restaurant and I said to her: 'Why don't you and I get together?' With genuine warmth and enthusiasm, she replied that she would love to. There was a brief pause, and she added, 'But I won't be able to. I've been called to the mountains and it's very important that I go there.'

"Having now had two dreams about a woman I hardly knew, I began to get intrigued. I decided to call her and arrange a meeting. As we hadn't exchanged numbers, and I didn't recollect ever having heard her last name, I was unable to look her up in the telephone directory. The only course of action was to call my acquaintance, Bill, and ask for her number. I felt awkward about doing that, though, and so I left it.

"That night, for the third time in a row, I dreamt of Anne again. In the dream, a voice said: 'Anne's last name is Heath.' I woke up feeling spooked. 'If I find her under that name in the directory,' I told myself, 'then something very bizarre is happening.' So I looked up her name in the Ojai telephone directory, but I couldn't find a listing. I felt a mixture of disappointment and relief.

"Now my curiosity was on fire, and so I called Bill to get her number. I rang her and explained to her that I'd had a dream about searching for someone and had been told in the dream that the person's name was Anne. I asked her if she'd like to get together for a chat. She replied that she would love to, but (I held my breath, waiting to see if she'd say she had to go to the mountains) she was about to leave for Zaca Lake, in the Santa Ynez Valley, north of Santa Barbara (a mountainous area, I observed to myself with satisfaction). 'However,' she went on, 'I could meet you now, if you're free.'

"She met me on the coffee shop patio. I went there with out any preconception about what our relationship,

27

if any, might be; I was happy for it to unfold naturally. During our talk, she told me she was an intuitive healer, and I wondered whether that would be the dimension in which an exchange would take place. She gave me her card, which read:

INTUITIVE HEALING
& TRAINING SESSIONS
Anne Heath

"I stared at the card in confusion. The name I had been given in my dream was Heath. I couldn't believe it.

"Anne told me a little about Zaca Lake, a place I'd often heard talked about but had never visited. In Chumash Indian, she explained, the name meant 'healing waters.' According to the Chumash, Zaca was the other end of the rainbow from Ojai. She said that the Chumash were fiercely monogamous and whenever there was marital discord the couple would travel to Zaca Lake in order to find peace.

"That night I dreamt of Anne again. I met her in the park, and I went straight up to her and kissed her on the lips. I remember wondering if she would accept this or not. She did.

"A few days later she called me from Zaca Lake and we made an arrangement for me to visit her. I went up there on March 20th and, as I drove along the

101 freeway north of Santa Barbara, I learned from the radio that this was the first day of spring. I was surprised because I thought spring always started on the 21st.

"It was a glorious day. Yellow and purple flowers lined the freeway and the ocean was still and blue. A squadron of pelicans patrolled the shoreline, watched over by a couple of wandering cumulus clouds. A faint breeze stirred the eucalyptus trees.

"I felt totally relaxed and quietly confident that everything would turn out OK. But my heart was beating fast, nevertheless.

"North of Buellton, I left the freeway and traveled for six or seven miles on a narrow lane winding through prestigious vineyards—Firestone, Zaca Mesa and Foxgen. Then I came across the enormous stone entranceway Anne had given as a landmark. It seemed to draw my car into it like a rocky funnel swallowing water. I opened the combination lock on the gate and drove cautiously along the twisting road. Five times I had to cross the creek and each time the car's fan belt squealed like a pig. Each side of the road were green meadows carpeted with purple lupins.

"As I approached Zaca Lake, I saw that it was located in a deep bowl of mountains covered with pine trees. I was struck immediately by the hushed serenity of the place. It was entirely plausible that the Chumash would view it as a healing spot.

"At the far side of the lake was the main lodge, and a little further around the lake a dozen cabins were scattered among the trees.

"I met Anne at the lodge. She was chatting animatedly with a woman called Lucy who was planning to open up a metaphysical store in the Danish-style village of Solvang, about twenty miles away. Anne hugged me enthusiastically.

"We drove to her cabin and she went inside to change, so that we could go for a hike around the lake. I sat at a picnic table in front of the cabin and stared at the building and the trees surrounding it. A shiver ran down my spine: I had never been here before, and yet I was now in a place that was identical to one of the scenes in my dream. Anne came out wearing black leggings and white sneakers. The sun caught her hair, just as it had done in the dream.

"We strolled around the lake, joking about this and that. I was happy to discover that she had a good sense of humor, and I felt at ease in her presence. Then we took a canoe out on the lake. She sat in the front and I sat in the back, and we paddled gently across the water. Schools of catfish lurked near the water's edge watched by statuesque herons. Randomly around the lake there would be a splash of water and I'd catch an explosion of orange out of the corner of my eye—carp were surfacing to feed on hovering insects. The sun was low and the vegetation around the lake was suffused in a deep yellow glow.

"I felt my heart melting as we glided softly through the water. The synchronization of our paddling, the single unit formed by Anne, me and the canoe, the sight of her proudly straight back and her leonine hair, created a profound sense of familiarity in me, as though we had been harmonious partners many times, in many lifetimes. If this story ends (and I don't know if it does) with Anne and I as mates, then this first day of spring at Zaca Lake—the air almost dripping with life, joy and hope—will be the moment I first fell in love with her. I was just too bemused to know it.

"When we had docked the canoe, Anne suggested climbing the hill to a gazebo that looked out over the valley. We scrambled up the steep hillside and walked breathlessly into the gazebo. We leaned on the railing and admired the view. Then we looked down at the railing and saw an inscription engraved on the wood—it was the names 'Jay' and 'Anne' surrounded by a heart. No doubt it was a coincidence, but there was an eerieness about it that made my flesh tingle. Anne looked at me inquiringly and I grinned at her, a little

31

embarrassed. It all seemed so intimate, for two people who scarcely knew each other.

"When the sun set, it became cold and we retreated to her cabin and lit a fire. She fetched a bottle of cabernet sauvignon from the lodge, together with a loaf of seven-grain bread, a slab of bright white goat's cheese, homemade chunky pesto and a bowl of local black olives. We sat on her bed, eating and drinking and talking about astrology. Not surprisingly, she was very well versed in the subject.

"When she learned I was an Aquarian, she told me about her first love. It had been a rare one—a boy she had known from the age of eleven to twenty. He had been her companion throughout those intensely formative years of adolescence. I felt deep affection for this person who had been there faithfully for Anne during such a critical period. She told me he was very brilliant, visionary and totally ungrounded. 'The way you seem to be,' she added, scrutinizing me with an amused expression on her face. 'Around the time of his birthday, I felt this strange longing for him. It was so intense I began a search for him through the Internet, but without success. That was last month. His birthday was February 4th, 1953. When's yours?'

"I stared at her. 'February 4th, 1953,' I replied.

"The evening continued and I still wondered what the truth of things was between us. It still seemed possible that we were being connected for reasons to do with work or healing, and that any passing romantic thoughts were the fruit of an overactive imagination.

"Then Anne rose to put another log on the fire. As she turned back toward me, I put my arm out tentatively. She could have ignored it and I could have converted the action into an innocuous stretch. But she didn't ignore it. She came to me and we kissed, and it was the softest, sweetest kiss imaginable. We lay on the bed for hours kissing, and in between kisses I told her the complete story of all my dreams.

"Later in the evening we dozed a little. Our lips were still touching and the mingling of our breaths into one seemed to my semiconscious mind like the most exquisite experience of my life.

"We got up at midnight. We went to the kitchen in the lodge and made tea. Anne became Anne again —this vibrant, separate, complex, mysterious being who, when I look one way, seems like somebody I have known forever, and when I look another way seems like a total stranger.

"Once I was fortified with tea, I drove back to Ojai. As I maneuvered the car along the winding mountain roads, I reflected deeply on my life. I saw that I had always been terrified of losing a loved one, of becoming destitute, of being forced to eke out a living in a humiliating way, of failing, of being betrayed sexually, of being an outcast. I realized that, during the last few years, I had been called upon to face every single one of these fears. And I understood that the collapse I had experienced was not a punishment but a cure; for it had been the collapse of a life built on fear.

"I arrived in Ojai just in time to begin folding news-papers at dawn in the supermarket parking lot. I could barely see the papers, for my eyes were filled with tears. A loving energy had shaped my dreams, worked miracles of synchronicity and brought me, with a fan-fare, to Anne. In a secret place inside me, deeper than proof, I knew this was a sign—a sign that I was ready to begin a new life; a life aligned with my spirit; a life expressive of my true nature; a life built on love. My tears, dropping silently on three hundred copies of the *Ventura County Star,* were born of relief and gratitude."

The Miracle of Patience is that it allows our heart's desires to manifest. Once Jay had surrendered to the collapse of his dreams, his life started to unfold according to its own rhythm, and the treasures awaiting him began to be revealed.

Patience is cradled in the faith that there is a hidden intelligence working for our highest good, whereas impatience is the imposition of our will and knowledge onto a grander scheme. When we are impatient we cling proudly to what we know, and so we remain imprisoned in our habitual lives. Patience, on the other hand, creates an opening through which unknown splendors may appear.

Are we ready to see that our self-willed, impatient ambition has never served us well? Has the time come for us to embrace the qualities of allowing, faith and patience, realizing that they support the highest vision we have of ourselves?

"Nothing can bring you serenity but yourself."

Proverb

SHATTERED IN THE CANYON
Serenity

Angela's life was blossoming in all areas, when Fate came around a corner and smashed her body and her dreams. Drawing on a profound understanding of the miracle of serenity, she was able to accept her tragedy and ultimately find the blessings contained within it.

"I REMEMBER very clearly the day of your accident," I tell Angela. "I was up in the canyon in the afternoon getting my house ready for a party that evening. Around 4:30 P.M. I heard a cacophony of sirens and later on a helicopter flew overhead. It seemed strange, because it wasn't the fire season, but I couldn't imagine what else an emergency of that scale could be about.

"My guests showed up at six, and I was being bubbly and sociable, when Andy called. He gave me the news and I was stunned. I had this awful, shocked pain inside me, and I was trembling as I returned to the party. Friends asked me what was wrong, and I told them. We gathered some candles together and placed them in the center of the room. We then sat in a circle and prayed. Everybody was overwhelmed by concern for you and by a dreadful sense of the fragility of life.

"I kept thinking, 'Why Angela, of all people? Why this phenomenally attractive aerobics and yoga instructor, this perfect physical specimen?'

"So I hope there were dimensions to this horror you can tell me about that will allow us to salvage a sense of a benevolent universe, because otherwise we have to talk about an evil universe, don't we? A universe that would smash a beautiful person without there being any upside to it."

Angela smiles. Even though it is two-and-a-half years since the accident, multiple jaw fractures, pulverized bones around her left eye and a crushed cheek mean that even a simple smile is an achievement. "I guess I have to start philosophically," she says. "Five years ago, when Andy's and my house burnt down, I learned that there are no all good or all bad experiences. That kind of labeling just doesn't make sense. Within twenty-four hours we had fifteen places to stay, offers of garages full of furniture and an outpouring of love and support. We lost a lot materially, but we gained a lot spiritually and emotionally.

"Growth comes from these edge experiences. I wouldn't wish my accident on anybody because it's physical torture—seventy fractures, according to one doctor's estimate, in twenty-four different bones—but there's no question that it was a catalyst for inner growth. For example, I was immediately reconnected to my intuition. I've always been intuitive, but I had distanced myself from it. If I spoke from my intuition I would qualify it. I'd say, 'I know this sounds weird, but …'. I was trying to grow in that area, to own my natural intuition and not question it. After the accident, one of the first things I noticed was that I was speaking from my intuition with no qualifiers or questioning. I was really touching people—almost doing readings for them. I was immersed in spirit. I really had that sense about me, and almost everybody who visited me in the hospital commented on it."

Angela's old Mercedes crumpled in the collision and she was trapped in the twisted metal. When the fire-fighters had extricated her, she was flown by helicopter to the county hospital, was stabilized and then transported to Cedars-Sinai Medical Center, one of the world's most prestigious hospitals. For fifteen days she was conscious but unable to retain memories. She would ask where she was, what had happened, and where her dog, Buddy, was. They would tell her she had been in a car accident and that Buddy was fine. Then a few minutes later she would ask the same questions over again.

When she recovered her short-term memory and could register the information given by the medical staff and her family, she still had no memory of the accident. "Nobody had told me I was trapped," she says. "They all thought it was a good thing if I couldn't remember that."

The memory, however, returned with alarming abruptness one day while she was attempting to brush her teeth. A friend, who was assisting her, jogged the hospital tray so that it pushed against her and the mirror she was looking in snapped shut. The next thing she knew she was reliving the accident and screaming to be let out. The pressure of the tray against her chest and the bed against her back, together with the loud bang of the mirror, had unlocked the frozen memory.

She remembered driving down the narrow country road and experiencing the explosive surge of adrenaline at the sight of an oncoming car taking the curve in the middle of the road; and, although the moment of impact was still wiped from her memory, she recalled being trapped in the car and remembered her terrified screams for help. Her last memory was of Sherman, her neighbor and friend who had been first on the scene of the accident, touching her shoulder. He was pulling the car seat back to relieve the pressure on her body. "I'm in the car with you," he reassured her, "and I won't leave until you do. Help is on the way. They're going to get you out." Then she lost consciousness.

"When I became conscious enough to register it," Angela tells me, without any trace of self-pity, "the pain was excruciating. I can't even describe it. No quantity of morphine was enough to eat up that amount of agony. They'd have had to kill me.

"But pain, both physical and emotional, is a part of life, and if we can accept it and embrace it and go into it, we discover it's there for a reason. We're in a culture that wants to push away from anything that we've labeled bad or scary and in so doing we've created a split and closed the door on half of life's experience, as if it had nothing to teach us. Life's challenges are much harder to handle with an attitude of rejection. What we reject seems to get stronger rather than go away.

"I saw this clearly with the physical pain. The way I dealt with it was by leaning into it. By actually floating in it, it was much easier to handle. Resistance is the natural tendency, but the tension it creates adds to the pain. Acceptance eases it.

"When I regained awareness in the hospital, the thought crept in: 'Why did this happen to me?' Then I said to myself, 'Well, I get that one: I was going down the road and this car came around a curve on the wrong side and hit me, and that's why it happened.

41

Simple!' The next question was 'What? What can I do with this?' And I realized that acceptance was the key.

"During the preceding ten years, I had often contemplated the serenity prayer—you know, asking for serenity to accept the things you cannot change, the courage to change the things you can, and the wisdom to know the difference. I knew if I didn't accept the accident, I'd get stuck. I'd become caught in the experience; it would become my identity. I saw how easily I could curl up on the sofa and never uncurl again. I knew that I could just survive or choose to thrive. I had been handed 'Victimhood' on a silver platter and I decided not to take it.

"After reflecting on this, I was immediately confronted with a test. I was thirsty and tried to take a sip of water by myself, but found I couldn't make even a simple movement like that. In that moment when I was powerless to change anything physically, I drew inspiration from the serenity prayer: I saw clearly that there *was* something I could change—my perception of the situation and my attitude, which is all we really have anyway. I knew that I could choose to accept what had happened, without being a victim, and that I could choose a path of healing.

"As I lay there, unable to do anything for myself physically, another insight came to me. I began to take stock of the situation, and I realized that what I was flipping through in my memory bag was not every fascinating, wonderful, joyous thing that ever happened to me; instead, every difficult, hard experience I ever went through came to mind. Past adversities became my tool bag. In that moment I became grateful for all the challenges I'd ever had in my life. I could draw from them the wisdom I needed to get through this. They helped me find that place of serenity and acceptance."

"I don't think many of us would have been capable of that," I comment. "It must have taken quite exceptional courage to accept the situation."

"It wasn't courage," Angela replies. "It was choice. It was making the choice to live. I understood that I had to actively choose life. For a few months before the accident, I had been in a place where I had been thanking God for life. Even though I still had problems, they were quality ones. I had spent the last year recovering from a financially catastrophic divorce, but now my business was working, I was doing projects I loved, everything I had ever dreamed of was happening, and I had been waking up grateful for months. I think that helped me get through it. It helped me make that choice to live. I don't view that as courage— courage seems somehow too personal and self-glorifying.

"It may sound strange, but I don't consider what happened as being entirely personal—it wasn't just my accident. I have a friend, Bear Watcher, who's an Apache medicine man, and he talks of the unity in life—it's a web, and some things touch the web and really shake it hard, and we all feel it when that happens."

"Like Lady Diana's death or Christopher Reeves's horse riding accident," I suggest.

"I wouldn't want to compare myself with them," Angela replies with a laugh. "But in a small way, in our town, my accident was like that. It touched different places on the web. I was a normal, average part of our community. It could have been the girl next door. For some it was the girl next door! Many people were affected in this way."

I recall the candlelight vigil in the park, where one-hundred-and-fifty friends gathered to pray for her recovery. I think of the hundreds of people who crowded into an auditorium, at $200 a head, to be part of a benefit concert performed by a rock star who lived locally. I remember how, for a while, our habitual pettiness subsided and we united.

I tell her this, and she says: "After the accident, I got to see the God in everybody. They were my angels— they helped me. It taught me a lot about judgment. I was reminded that we all contain dark and light. When something comes up from our shadow side, it doesn't mean we're not still loving, giving, wonderful, good people. I give other people, and myself too, a lot more space for all the 'shadow stuff.' It's part of being human, and I don't judge it in the way I used to.

"Another result of the accident was that it gave me an insight into the fact that everything's a question of perspective. At first, my focus was on healing my left eye, even if basic motion detection was the best that could be hoped for. Then I developed a rare condition called sympathetic opthalmia. (This means the immune system, which is attacking the scar tissue in the injured eye, accidentally attacks the healthy eye.) Now the focus shifted to not going blind. Healing became saving my seeing eye, and losing the injured one suddenly changed from being a disaster into being an indispensable feature of the healing process.

"The accident also brought me into the now. It gave me a very important realization, which is that there is no such thing as 'later.' 'Later' is just a construct. Life is a lot of nows strung together. 'Later' never happened for me. I never got to the bank, which is where I was heading. I never went to dance class that evening. I never finished creating the program for the fundraising event I was organizing, and I never made the breakfast meeting scheduled for the next day. My finances and business plans were in ruins. All my pictures of 'later' were shattered, along with my body, in the canyon.

"All I had left was the fact of being alive. Although that may not sound like much, it is, in reality, everything. Despite daily chronic pain, which could continue my whole life, the accident put me in touch with the most profound sense of gratitude for my life. If you were looking for a saving grace, Jonathan, I'd say that was it. I was shown the infinite preciousness of simply being alive."

The Miracle of Serenity *is that it allows us to see reality. The mind is like a beautiful pond: when agitated it is opaque, when calm it is translucent.*

Serenity is a quality we think we value, but actually we don't. We doubt its effectiveness in most of the situations in our lives. Paradoxically, we are more likely to recognize its virtues when, like Angela, we are in extremis. But when it's after midnight and our teenager still isn't home, few of us view serenity as a useful state of mind. And that is a mistake, because serenity is effective, while anxiety is not. Emotional tension limits our range of responses, whereas serenity expands us, so that the universe's infinitely creative intelligence can float elegant solutions into our minds.

Serenity doesn't mean we lack energy; our actions may be infused by intense passion. But the passion will flow from integrity and balance, from a deep understanding of the truth of a situation. It will not be the discordant energy that motivates neurotic action. It's hard for us to see this, because we have been so heavily conditioned into believing that anxiety denotes caring and that it impels effective action. And that is why it is so difficult to let go of stress and anxiety—we won't give up harmful behavior as long as we mistakenly believe it benefits us.

Therefore, our first task is to see that the strategy of anxiety does harm us, in every situation. When we see this

47

deeply, we will drop the strategy. As we do so, serenity—which is an intrinsic quality—will arise naturally. And then we will see with new eyes, and we will find blessings everywhere, even in the midst of tragedy.

"On what instrument are we strung?

What player holds us in His hand?"

Rilke

HARP MAGIC
Harmony

> The events in our lives can seem disconnected. We meet people and do things and there is no synergy. But then angels of inspiration visit us, and we see that everything that happens is in the service of the Cosmic Song. There is a miraculous harmony underlying all of life.

IT IS A DROWSY, warm Sunday afternoon. I am sitting on the patio at Local Hero, an Ojai bookstore and coffee shop. It's a good place. There's caring behind it—a love of books, a love of music and art, a love of fine tastes and smells. It's more than just a business, it's a gift to the community that comes straight from the heart. You can tell—look in Bobby Huston, the owner's, eyes. Beneath the shifting patterns of surface emotions, you can see his inner beauty and his kindness.

I am with a friend, Maria Hemingway. We are sponsoring an evening in Ojai with Neale Donald Walsch, whose book, *Conversations with God,* is securely ensconced at the top of the bestseller list. We are discussing the arrangements for Neale's visit.

A friend of Maria's is about to play the harp. Maria whispers to me that his name is Peter Sterling and that he channels music from angels. I watch him as he sets up the instrument. His movements are precise and calm. He seems quietly at ease and very centered. He positions himself at the harp, flexes his fingers and then begins to play music that is … angelic.

The notes tumble out in melodic waves that resonate in every part of me. They caress my mind and quiet it; soften my heart and open it; whisper to my soul in its own language and soothe it. I can feel my body relaxing. A sweet, healing energy flows through me. I become very still and clear, and into this stillness the words "Ask Peter to open the evening with Neale Donald Walsch" drift like sailboats across a calm sea.

During the intermission, Maria introduces me as the person cosponsoring Neale's talk. I compliment Peter on his playing and am about to broach the subject of his opening for Neale, when he interjects: "Perhaps you'd like me to play at Neale Walsch's talk." Taken aback, I lamely reply that it's a wonderful idea. He adds: "It came into my mind when I was playing the second piece." Wow! My wits return to me. Excitedly, I tell him that the idea popped into my mind, too, at exactly the same moment. A special feeling is exchanged between us —I know we'll be friends.

Later, we meet at the Ojai Coffee Roasting Company and Peter tells me his story.

"It started when I moved to Sedona, Arizona, in 1990, after I had been living in Colorado for ten years. I had been a ski instructor, spending almost every day up on the slopes above Aspen, skiing in the rarefied atmosphere of the Rockies. As I flew down the mountainside I had a vision of living a different kind of life. I had always had a sense of being a creative artist and I always wanted to pursue that dream. I knew I had to leave Colorado and find a creatively uplifting place that would nourish me spiritually. I felt strongly guided to move to Sedona.

"I was used to listening to my inner voice. As a young boy, I had a grandmother who repeatedly urged me to pay attention to it. The voice was faint, but audible, and over time I began to trust it, although sometimes it's led me into places that to this day I still doubt—it's taken me along strange, less-traveled roads, for as yet unexplained reasons.

"Once I moved to Sedona, people soon came into my life who had very different lifestyles from mine. They lived clean, healthy, spiritual lives, and they became my teachers. I loved hanging out with them—learning about

53

myself, how to take care of myself, how to cleanse my body and have an experience of clarity.

"Under the influence of these new friends, I changed my diet—I became vegetarian and started eating sprouts and live foods. I also met a chiropractor who was a very talented healer and a shaman. I had sessions with him five times a week, and he would do incredible things to me—a skillful application of chiropractic practices, herbs, tinctures and sounds.

"At this time, I was living in my van in the canyons outside Sedona. It is an extraordinary wilderness area—very powerful energetically. As I explored these canyons I noticed a marvelous silence there and an incredible presence. I began to spend time sitting on brick-red rocks by gurgling creeks, meditating. As I progressively allowed my mind to quiet, I began to hear what seemed to me the sounds of some kind of celestial music, an angelic choir. My hearing began to alter so I could perceive more—instead of the third eye opening it was as if a third ear was opening.

"The music was orchestral, with strings and choir, on a stupendously grand scale, grander than anything I've heard on earth. Many mystics have talked about this—the music of the spheres.

"Around this time, I began to feel that this music was wanting to come out of me. It needed to flow through me and be expressed. I had never mastered an instrument before, although I'd always been musically inclined and had a good ear for music. I had this musical talent bottled up in me, but I hadn't found an instrument with which to express it. Finally, after thirty-two years, as I listened to this inner music in the Arizona wilderness, I discovered what my instrument would be—the harp.

"Immediately, synchronistic events started to take place. A woman had a small Celtic harp she wanted to sell, so she let me try it and at once there was a recognition. It was almost like a cosmic connection. The universe cheered and said, "Yes, he's found his instrument." It felt really right, and so I ended up purchasing the harp for a few hundred dollars.

"This led me into a period where I was very much impassioned and obsessed with the harp. The instrument had a small little carrying case and each day I would go into the wilderness and play for four or five hours. I'd hike back into the canyons and find a magical place and play for the wind and the rocks and the little animals that lived there.

"I took a couple of lessons from the woman—how to hold the harp and how it worked—but then I just taught myself. I felt that I knew how to do this, and that something was trying to happen through me. Within the first few weeks of playing, this melody started to

55

come through, sort of a recognized feeling. I was hearing the inner music and at the same time the music was harmonizing with the harp. I realized that there was some form of energy around me, working through me, and thought it must be angels.

"It was around the time of my birthday, and I climbed to the top of a ridge above a canyon and I held my harp up in prayer. I said: 'I know you're with me. I'm ready to receive the gift of this music and I offer myself up as a vessel for it.'

"It was as if they had been waiting for my permission. I sat down and surrendered myself to this powerful force, and began to play. I was totally relaxed and my hands began moving as if I was a concert harpist, as though I had been playing all my life—it came through that strong. My fingers were playing by themselves with a virtuosity that I had been totally incapable of until that moment. It was such a powerful force. So much love and light was coming through that tears were flowing from my eyes.

"I began to connect more and more with what I perceived as angels playing through me. I increasingly listened to my inner voice, and it seemed that they were communicating with me, telling me that I was to work with them to bring through this celestial music. At first it seemed so far out that I didn't really understand or believe it. Sometimes I would sit in front of a mirror and play, just to convince myself that I really was playing—it was such a unique experience I couldn't believe it was happening.

"After a while, I asked the angels to show themselves to me. One of the first times I saw them, I was playing at sunrise in the forest. I was walking back to my van and I saw a light hovering above it, about the size of a fist. I blinked my eyes, doing a double take, and as I began to look at it, it got very excited and began to move rapidly back and forth. It did that for a few seconds and then shot up over my head and flew away. It was like a Tinkerbell kind of thing.

"Each time now, when I went out and played in the power spots and vortexes around Sedona, I would ask them to appear for me. I would perceive shimmering light around me and they would begin to take on a form. At night I would see them much more clearly. I would see them flying around in front of my face, leaving little trails like fireflies. There was a whole swarm of them and they would begin to dance in front of my eyes. Slowly they became distinct, and I saw that they were little cherubs, such as you would see on the Sistine Chapel.

"I still perceive them to this day. They're with us now. They like it when we talk about them. You can

57

catch them out of the corner of your eye. You can't see them with your three-dimensional eyes, though; they're in a different dimension"

I look around me. I can see nothing, and yet there is something so calm and sane about Peter that I have no doubt he is telling the truth.

"One of the things I liked to do was to hold out my finger and have them alight on the tip of it. They would hover on my fingertips, looking at me, and I could make out their faces and wings, and I could tell they were holding harps. They were celestial musicians.

"After a few months of playing this celestial music, I was guided to Byron Bay in Australia. I met a talented musician there who had a recording studio, and my guidance from the angels was to work with this guy and record some of the melodies that were coming through. So I did that, and I played the songs, and he added strings and flute and we made a tape.

"I remember walking along the beach at Byron Bay. It was a beautiful place with a subtropical rain forest coming down to a crescent-shaped golden beach that stretched for about ten miles. Dolphins and whales were playing just off the shoreline. As I walked there, listening to the recording on my Walkman, my inner vision opened up, as if projected onto a screen, and I saw myself going back to America and recording an album as a professional harpist. They showed me the whole thing. They showed me the actual CD and that it was in a catalog and that the right people were going to show up to market it. It was all going to be taken care of.

"I moved back to Sedona from Australia and bought a bigger harp. I played it for about a month, and then I got the message that it was now time for me to make another recording. So I booked a studio. Before my session I said a prayer and asked for the music to come through clearly. I got into the studio and this powerful energy came into me from the angels and I played from my heart for about an hour-and-a-half. Almost the whole time my hands were moving by themselves. My eyes were teary, so most of the time I couldn't see what I was doing. Some musicians turned up who donated their talent and played some guitar and keyboard. And by the end of it (I worked on the recording for about a month) I had a little cassette containing eight songs. I colored the cassette labels myself and gave them to a few friends and also put them in the bookstores in Sedona.

"In this way, I began to promote and market my cassette, but it was difficult for me to make the phone calls and put the necessary business energy into it. So I prayed to the angels and told them that if they wanted this music to go out, I needed help. I did a little ceremony and a ritual and then I let go of it.

59

"About a week later, I got a phone call from a record company. One of their executives had been on vacation in Sedona and had heard my tape playing in a bookstore. He found my number on the label, called me up, and offered me a recording contract. I could hardly believe that it was happening and that the angels had worked so swiftly and effectively.

"I signed a contract with the company for five albums over five years. They digitally re-mastered my cassette and pressed a CD out of it. We called the album *Harp Magic,* put a nice cover on it and started distributing it all over the world. Three weeks after it was released it was nominated for a national award—NAIRD, the National Association of Independent Record Distributors. It's like a baby Grammy award; what Sundance is to the Academy Awards.

"Many incredible things began to happen. I would get letters from people who would write me and tell me that the angels had healed them with the music, how it had helped them through difficult times. I really believe the angels' energy is present on that record, and that you can have a direct experience of it.

"So it's been quite a journey and I'm still on it. A lot of people are having angel experiences all over the world now. I think it's happened at other times, at critical junctures of human history. The angels come as our brothers to help us through difficult transitions. They influence us with their love and inspire us to go for the light and to go for love.

"The music has that frequency in it. It can heal people, open their hearts, create great visions in their imagination. It can inspire them to reach for something higher."

When Neale Walsch came to Ojai, Peter played his harp for half an hour before the start of the talk; but members of the audience were chatting with each other and not paying much attention. When Peter had finished, Neale took the stage, and then called Peter back; he invited him to play an accompaniment to a guided meditation. This time, the audience was so attentive you could hear a pin drop. In the stillness, a new, palpable presence could be felt. There was a sense of new energies arriving—a gathering of angels, perhaps.

The Miracle of Harmony is elucidated in this ancient story:

Once there was a spiritual seeker who was told of a well that was inhabited by a spirit. This spirit could reputedly answer the question: "What is the Truth?"

Thrilled, the seeker journeyed to the well to receive illumination. The spirit told him to visit a nearby village. "At the crossroads," it explained, "You will find what you are looking for."

So the seeker went to the crossroads but, when he got there, all he found were three tiny shops. Inside the first there were scraps of metal heaped in piles; inside the second, there were pieces of wood; and inside the third there were bits of wire of little value.

The seeker rushed back to the well and demanded an explanation. But all that came back to him was the echo of his voice and the reflection of his angry face in the water.

For ten years he wandered the land, until one day, while sitting under a banyan tree, he heard the most enchanting sounds he had ever known. Mesmerized, he followed the sounds until he reached a clearing. And in the clearing he came upon a sight that caused him to yell for joy—everything he had seen at the crossroads in the village now made sense. The scraps of metal were frets and braces, the lengths of wire were strings, and the pieces of wood were the sounding board: all the *disparate components had been fashioned into a sitar, which was being played by a master musician. As the wondrous, perfectly harmonious music stilled the seeker's mind, he sunk into the infinite sweetness of his own being.*

"We know what we are, but not what we may be."

Shakespeare

TRANSFORMING GRIEF TO THE ELEVENTH POWER
Creativity

Though the creative impulse can be destructive, bursting relentlessly through our crustiness, it is also a healing force. In this story, creative energy transforms Susan's grief into love. But the benefits of this energy are not for her alone: her art now touches the hearts of people around the world and helps them heal. This is the miracle of pure creativity.

WE ARE SITTING on the deck of Susan's little cottage, hidden from the world in the middle of an immense orange grove. Susan rolls a cigarette expertly, filling it with American Spirit natural tobacco. Charcoal in the barbecue is crackling and smoking. She shakes a jar of Greek olives into an earthenware bowl, and then deftly withdraws a cork from a bottle of Merlot. The food, the drink, the tobacco, the sting of smoke in our eyes—it feels indigenous; we're ready to talk our good talk.

When she was twenty-nine, I learn, Susan started up an art school for little children; she moved into a nearby loft and felt content with her life. It was not long, however, before she started to have strange dreams that lasted for hours, dreams that were an eerie mixture of waking and sleeping images. She saw a group of lost young men, wearing only towels around their waists, pacing about her room; she kept hearing that it was her job to help them, to give them a purpose. A couple of days later she was gazing out of her loft at a deserted building down the street, when an unaccountable shiver ran through her. She inquired with the neighbors and discovered that the deserted building had been the public baths. Shortly before she arrived in the neighborhood, the baths had been gutted in an inferno, which had killed eleven gay men. It was they who had been in the loft with her.

At other times, in this strange waking-dreaming state, she saw past life experiences and other phenomena broadcast on her television. On one occasion a gnarly, hag-like Tibetan woman appeared, and the next day Susan was invited to a neighbor's house where Tibetan Buddhist prayers were being chanted. It was her first exposure to them, and yet she could recite them as if she had known them all her life. She felt a sudden reconnection with a lost part of herself. It was like coming home.

"Tibetan Buddhism awakened me to something vast," Susan tells me. "It was my introduction to the sacred; I had finally discovered a path for myself as a mystic. I found the practices incredibly powerful; I felt a deep connection with my teacher; and I experienced a love that was amazingly profound."

At the time, she was in a relationship with Gary, a man twelve years her senior. He had been a famous artist, and had graced the cover of *Life* magazine. He had worked in Boston with all the prestigious artists, poets and scientists. Timothy Leary, Ram Dass and Bob Dylan had been his best friends. Now, at the age of forty, he was an old beatnik who'd "been there, done of all that." He just wanted to relax and lead a quiet life.

One balmy day in October, after they had been together nine years, Susan was sitting with Gary by a stream in the Catskills. Gary's twenty-one-year-old son Adam, a shy and angelic young man, was with them. Susan was watching a pair of red maple leaves drop and float away in the water, when she suddenly heard angel voices. And what she heard them saying was so far removed from any thought she had ever had that she just sat there gaping. The voices were melodic, like music. They seemed to drift through the air to her, transported on the effervescent sounds of the stream. They were giving voice to the unthinkable: "You and Dave," they announced, "are destined to be together."

67

Dave? He was sixteen years her junior and she had no interest in him. Perhaps, she thought, it was a trick of her imagination. She determined not to mention it to the others. However, Gary had heard the voices too, and later that evening he broached the subject. He loved the idea. Susan had been unable to have a baby with him, and he thought that maybe with Dave she would. Dave was family; there'd be no problem. If she had a baby, they would all raise it together. The prospect delighted him. "I don't normally talk about this," Susan says. There is a long pause before she continues. "It took a whole year for me to be convinced. Finally, however, I agreed, and it was something I never regretted, even though it ended in tragedy. The relationship with Dave was out of this world, literally.

"We were already married on the inner plane. We were one. Our love was beyond belief. Nothing else mattered. It was the kind of love that would heal the world. The kind of love that was the beginning and end of every cell of my body, the fulfillment of a million lifetimes."

After four years with Dave and his father, Susan's life began to shift. The Tibetan Buddhism she had been practicing now seemed too confining for her. She was starting to have experiences that wouldn't fit Buddhist paradigms. She was having psychic incidents with storms, lightning and sunspot activity—reading them and getting prescient information that was later con-firmed. Then, animals started talking to her. She would think of an animal—a red fox, say—and it would instantly show up. She would receive a "hit" from it, an intuitive sense of the answer to whatever question she was asking.

At the same time, her relationship with Gary had reached a chronic state of deterioration. She had become tired of supporting him financially. She was willing to examine their patterns of codependency, but he wasn't. She had been working faithfully for two years to save the relationship, but she couldn't do it alone; she needed a commitment from him to grow emotionally which he was unwilling to give.

Not only had she drifted away from Tibetan Buddhism and grown beyond her relationship with Gary, but she also felt confined in New York. Her thoughts turned to the vast expanses of the West, and she and Dave finally screwed up their courage and announced to Gary that they were relocating to New Mexico—without him. They wished to start a new life there on a farm.

Their new life in the West was short-lived, however. With hindsight, Susan recognizes that the seeds of madness were in Dave all along. He had told her once that he could remember his birth, and that he'd been

69

sent to this planet on a mission: he had come to save the world.

"I was a grounded, sane person," Susan says, and then whispers: "But, you know what? I believed him. I know it's hard to understand. But then I too have a memory of other realms, and so what he was saying made perfect sense to me. And Dave also was a truly wise being. He was simple, unschooled, and yet he had extraordinary insight.

"But, as I discovered later, there were also deeply disturbed sides to him. No sooner had we reached our dream farm in New Mexico and settled down there, than he began to have what appeared to be delusions. He became convinced that the government was onto him. He believed a secret government satellite was spying on us through our window.

"We shared the farm with a mother and her little boy Dave started to accuse the woman and her son of being antichrists. His madness finally became public when one day he tried to drag the kid into a vault so that he could be locked up and prevented from sabotaging Dave's 'mission.' The boy got scared and ran away, and Dave jumped into a car and chased him across the fields, attempting to capture him. The mother then chased after Dave—it was chaos, a nightmare—and finally the police were called. Dave and I were forced to leave the farm. We were lucky not to have been arrested."

So they were exiled out into the desert, where they lived for a few months in a trailer. "Why did I stay with him through all of this?" Susan muses. "I guess because I felt responsible for him and because I loved him so very much."

The episodes of madness continued, reaching a peak one night, when Dave woke Susan up, crying and laughing at the same time, saying: "It's happened! Oh my God it's happened!" He was hysterical. He claimed he'd had direct contact with his friends who'd sent him through the birth canal. They were watching him. One of them had actually entered his body and was looking through his eyes. They were now going to work with him to scan the physical environment to see what was good to keep in the New World and what needed to be discarded.

"He would do things," Susan says, "like sit for hours and scan a medicine cabinet. He had a mad look in his eyes. He was angry a lot and would rant and rave. He kept repeating that he had a mission to accomplish and that time was of the essence. He would stop people in the street and scare them." Weary of caring for a mad-man in the wilderness, feeling like she was in a war— forever on her guard, always fearful—and desperate for

71

the support of her friends, Susan convinced Dave to return to Woodstock. As they headed east, across the endless plains of Texas, pulling the trailer that had been their home for three months, Susan was crying with disappointment, humiliation and betrayal. Nothing was left of the life they had gone out West to create.

Dave was in a frenzy not knowing how to calm her down. He was driving and, from some awful impulse drawn from the depths of his disturbed psyche, he suddenly jerked the steering wheel; the trailer snapped and their car was flipped fifty feet into the air as in some gargantuan technological ballet. After nine somersaults, the car came to rest on the opposite side of the freeway. Dave, miraculously unharmed, pulled Susan out of the wreckage.

"As I was laying on the pavement," Susan tells me, "I had an incredible experience of serenity—finally I could stop and I could rest. I didn't have to handle any of this any more."

She spent ten days in the hospital and then returned with Dave to Woodstock for a lengthy convalescence. She had chipped a vertebra in her back, fractured two ribs, mangled her wrist and cracked her skull.

Once he was back home, Dave's state of mind became more subdued. He was quiet, helpful and loving. Susan's wrist required extensive and excruciating physiotherapy, and Dave acted as her therapist. There was a strangely calm atmosphere and the sweetest affection between them.

This continued for several months, until the tragedy. "The day before it happened," Susan tells me, "we had practiced some incredibly powerful ritualistic healing techniques, and I had felt myself transported to a place full of angels and light beings. Dave and I seemed to be in a pure realm together. The beings reassured us that everything was going to be fine. Given what happened the next day, however, I guess that was an illusion.

"I remember that day vividly. It was so tranquil. There was a new moon and we went to place crystals in the stream—the one where, four years before, our union had been foretold by angel voices. Then we went home and Dave helped me cook up some beets for borsch.

"While we were in the kitchen, there was a call from his mother saying their cat had died. It really hit Dave hard. She wanted him to go over and run some errands for her. I gave him sixty dollars to buy groceries, and he kissed me and said he'd hurry back. That's what we used to say to each other. 'Hurry back, hurry back.' I watched him walk to the car and I noticed something strange: normally he would turn around and wave to me before he left, but this time he didn't.

73

"The sun was going down. It was a very beautiful evening. I had a bottle of wine waiting for him and some candles burning. While I waited for him, I was studying our composite astrological charts. That's what I was doing while, unknown to me, he was dying.

"About the time he was due back, I heard a car door slam outside and I thought it was him. Then there was a second slam and I assumed he'd brought a friend home. I opened the front door and saw two cops approaching. They said: 'Did you guys have a fight?' I said I didn't understand. I could feel myself beginning to panic. It was the worst sensation of fear I've ever experienced, like a vice in my chest. They said, 'Your friend, Dave, is in the hospital. It doesn't look like he's going to survive.' I stared at them, not fully understanding their words.

"I found out later that Dave had sent his mother out shopping when he got to her house; that he had locked all the doors, written three notes—to me, to his mother and to the world—made a noose out of the dog leash, attached it to a beam, and hung himself.

"I was driven to the hospital; Dave was dead when I arrived. Two psychologists, specialists in suicide, were waiting for me. They insisted that I look at the body; they told me I would really regret it later if I didn't—so I did. As I looked at him, I didn't feel any rage, just love. I loved him so much. His neck was covered with a piece of cloth to conceal the awful burn mark left by the leash. I kissed him and told him I loved him. He was terribly white; he smelled of death."

Susan returned home with Gary and Dave's mother and a couple of friends, and sat in the living room all night in a daze. At about one o'clock in the morning a car crashed outside the house. A man came to the door and asked to use the phone. Outside, his red Nissan truck was wrecked—it was the exact color and make as Dave's. It was as though Dave's act of violence had created a field of distortion that was attracting surrealistic synchronicities.

"I knew that his death would either kill me or make me," Susan says quietly. "I decided it would make me—not just for me, but for all the generations of women in my family.

"As a therapy, I began typing, spewing out reams and reams of paper. One day, while I was typing, the sentence *This is Balthazar* appeared on the paper. I started to feel his presence—I felt myself expanding, as though I'd been given laughing gas. He became one of my guides.

"Then other psychic phenomena occurred. I met Karen G., a renowned medium and, while we were chatting, she suddenly said, 'I don't know if you want my medium skills, but there is somebody who wants to

75

talk to you big time.' It was Dave. I was now able to communicate with him. He told me how much he loved me and how sorry he was.

"It was around this time that I started working with the emotional states. I said to myself, 'Go inside and start trusting.' I began to be present in my body with the emotion, without reacting to it—just allowing it to run through, feeling the love in it. There's a lot of darkness when you're experiencing pain, but if you feel the emotion without judging it, mentalizing it ('I'm feeling grief'), or processing it—if you just let it be there—that's love.

"My first piece of cathartic art was *Transforming Grief to the Eleventh Power*. I drew it purely by instinct, not judging it. As I drew it, I felt myself lifting, becoming more and more in a state of love. I realized the art was healing me. By the end, I had truly transformed my grief —into love.

"Still, I was not sure where I was supposed to go with all this until one day I received a strange phone call from a friend. She told me she had dreamed that she was in an airport and that she'd heard over the loud-speaker: 'Susan, this is Balthazar. We're waiting for you. We have your project. You have twenty minutes.'

"After the call, I sat and meditated. All I had in my being at that time was grief and loss. Within a few minutes of sitting quietly, I began to receive instructions.

I was told that *Transforming Grief to the Eleventh Power* was to he followed by a series of drawings: fear, anger, trauma, anguish, aloneness and alienation; this series would be concluded with a drawing of 'Unconditional Love,' which I have yet to complete.

"So this has become my path. I remain present with an emotion and the hieroglyph design that corresponds to it appears on my inner screen. Then I draw it.

"It has been a path of healing. The drawings enable me to perform spiritual alchemy—transforming base, painful emotions into love. The art has also helped heal me by giving me something to do, giving me a purpose, a reason to live. And the drawings can be therapeutic for other people too. I have many friends who hang them on their walls and say they feel their transforming power."

Susan rolls another American Spirit cigarette and drinks from the glass of wine that she has been neglecting while telling her story. Her cat, Galaxy, is copying her: she is lapping up water from an ornate, long-stemmed goblet.

During the pause, I reflect on what she has told me. She strikes me as being a grounded person, very solid at her core, and yet I wonder to what degree she is getting misled by her lively imagination, clothing paranormal phenomena in pictures that are mere fictions.

77

"Isn't there great danger in this?" I ask. "It's possible that you were led astray by malevolent forces that appeared benign." I tell her of a dear friend of mine who is completely uninformed in spiritual matters, but who has by far the most integrity, common sense, balance, decency and open-heartedness of anybody I know. "Surely there's value in just being simple." I say.

"Yes, there is," Susan replies. "And you're right—I've sometimes been misled, so I do have to learn to be discriminating. However, there have been countless occasions when, looking back, I see that my guidance had loving objectives. My interpretation of that guidance is really irrelevant. In the end, practical effectiveness is all that counts. Identifying the source of the inspiration for my drawings, for example, isn't important. All that matters is that they have the power to heal; they have been healing me, and they have helped heal others too. I think that's enough."

I ask her if she has made money with her art, if it has been of practical help in that way.

"I haven't made money yet," she replies. "I'm drawing on a trust fund, although it's running out fast. I've chosen a path that is offbeat and different, but it's time for me to do that without judging it. I have to let go of the fear that I can't support myself this way. It has required courage. The fear says: 'You won't be able to make a living and you don't even know how to waitress.' It has taken courage to follow my dream, no matter what."

I admire her courage. She has oodles of it. She also has integrity. She's taken a huge bite out of life, swallowing chunks of undigested horror, and she has moved through the experiences with evident compassion and sincerity of intent. No doubt she took on the pain for many reasons that will remain mysterious; however, it seems clear that one purpose was to learn the secrets of spiritual alchemy, the transformation of suffering into love.

Her artwork speaks for itself; I feel its power. And Susan herself is a fine example of its transformational potency; she is neither self-pitying nor depressed; her spiritual buoyancy and inner strength are tangible.

I think again about Balthazar, about angelic voices in streams and premonitory dreams, about what's real and what's illusion. And I wonder whether it really matters. In the end, we're all doing the best we can. Susan, like the rest of us, is aiming for greater understanding; sometimes she'll hit the target and sometimes she'll miss. That seems inevitable. What counts is that she is a truly sincere person, with a tremendous gift, and the potential to help the world heal.

I give Susan a warm hug goodbye and thank her for the many hours she's spent with me revealing intimate information that she rarely shares with anybody. "You've been very generous," I tell her.

"You're welcome," she replies.

"It'll come back to you," I say, unaware that my words are prophetic. "Though it's not always immediately apparent, there's a fairness in the universe. I trust in that."

The next day I go to the Ojai Institute, a study and retreat center based on the teachings of Krishnamurti. I feel a strong attraction to Jesi, a middle-aged woman from India. She has liquid eyes that draw me in and an aura of competence that intrigues me. I engage her in conversation and learn that she is here for one day before heading up to San Francisco. In a serene, lilting voice she tells me that she is in California to find art that she can export to India. She has galleries there and she works directly with architects and interior designers. She tells me she's in Ojai to take a break, but nevertheless she'd be interested to see some art.

"Do you happen to know any artists?" she asks me, and then adds: "I'm looking particularly for work that has been channeled or has a spiritual dimension."

A shiver runs through me. This seems too weird to he a simple coincidence. I tell her about Susan and her eyes light up. We rush around to Susan's cottage and I hold my breath while Jesi inspects the canvases. She is inscrutable and I start to feel nervous. Perhaps she doesn't like them. Susan, I can tell, is sensing that a genuine opportunity has arisen, and she's pacing around excitedly.

When Jesi has viewed everything, she sits down on a chair, still expressionless. Then a beautiful smile lights up her face. "These are really good," she finally announces. "Incredible energy. I think I might be able to help you, Susan."

I leave the two women together to discuss business details. A few days later, I receive two phone calls. One is from Jesi expressing her appreciation for the introduction to Susan; she has sent Susan's paintings by express mail to India and her partners are so impressed they have offered to pay Susan's expenses to come and visit them. The other call is from Susan, warmly thanking me for helping her.

"I think it was Balthazar at work," I say, teasingly.

She laughs. "Well, something was at work."

I hang up the phone and jump onto my bed. Like my daughter, Emily, when she scores a goal in soccer, I enthusiastically shout out: "Yes!"

The Miracle of Creativity is that it's our most intimate relationship with Spirit. Divine energy is healing energy; therefore, as Susan discovered, the act of creation is therapeutic.

Creating is as natural to us as breathing. When, like a tree dropping its leaves in winter, we stand unadorned, without self-consciousness, the Light enters us and we spontaneously create.

Then, whatever we create is beautiful, like the simple paintings splashed onto paper by young children or daubed onto rock by cavemen. Whatever we create is powerful, like The Diary of Anne Frank, written from a place of truth, not sophistication. Whatever we create is moving, like a peasant flute player in the Andes filling his stark valley with a sweet melancholy.

Sometimes our natural gifts sink out of sight in the stagnant beliefs we have soaked up like a sponge from our culture. Seeing this sets us free. Seeing that our vitality and well-being flow from an inner spring, not from outer phenomena, reconnects us with our source.

Creative energy is at the core of our being and so, as we express our true nature (whether in the arts, in business, in relationships or in play), we become effortlessly creative. We discover that our lives are in fact delightfully choreographed and that an exquisite harmony lies at the heart of all things.

"It is the Way of Heaven not to strive, and yet it knows how to overcome; not to speak, and yet it knows how to win a response."

Lao-Tse

A MARVELOUS GAME
Strength

The Source—the energy that sustains the universe— operates mysteriously. When we get a glimpse of its secret ways, as we do in this story, we see an awesome power in action, and a humorous one too. Strength works its magic in marvelous ways.

HE IS *essence de cool.* His charisma could be bottled and sold on Sunset Boulevard. A talented pianist and singer, he and his rock band play Beethoven's *Fifth* at 1000 watts. He bangs out the melody on steel drums and (provided you have an ounce of cool in you too) it makes your hair stand on end, it's so hauntingly right. His name is Mr. Rogers, Mike to his friends.

His Laurel Canyon home is a three-story museum of musical instruments from Bali, Tibet, India and every other cosmically inclined place on earth. The living room walls are adorned with pictures of Krishnamurti, interspersed with photos of Mike and Elizabeth Taylor entwined in a hug. He plays the Hollywood game, but you know where his true values lie. It's an irresistible combination—maximum fun, minimum phoniness.

He drives to Ojai in his "Mercedillac." The front of the car is a convertible Mercedes 450 SL, the back is a 1950s Cadillac, complete with absurdly ornate wings. The car is lime green. Back in Los Angeles, pedestrians approach and laugh or clap. Valets miraculously discover one last space in full parking lots, and take the keys with delight.

Mike exudes charisma. It's not just the three-quarter length silk Balinese suit and black bowler hat; nor is it simply the long blonde hair and soft blue eyes. Beyond the trappings there is a sense of mastery that fills a room, a feeling of being in the presence of somebody who knows how things work, who has both street smart and spiritual acumen. If you want to build a house, he'll know all the shortcuts through the inspection red tape; and if you want to experience the rising of your kundalini, he'll know which Inca pyramid to go and meditate on—and, of course, how to fly there inexpensively.

Still in his thirties, he is to all intents and purposes retired. He makes music, travels, throws parties, goes on retreats, writes and only occasionally has to dabble in practical affairs, such as hiring out his recording studio or collecting rents from a sprinkling of houses that he owns around Los Angeles.

It's midnight and we're in the Deer Lodge, a bar in the boonies where rock bands play on weekends and bikers come to get drunk and fight. Mike is dancing with the prettiest girl there. The barmaids are watching him. When he orders drinks, they fall all over themselves to be the one to serve him. They don't see his like around here very often and it's making their evening.

Mike spends the night in a luxury motel on the outskirts of town. The room is complimentary because the manager is his friend. In the morning we drink herbal tea in the coffeehouse. He shuns stimulants like coffee, partakes sparingly of alcohol and has been vegetarian for many years. Recently he cut out all animal products too. "Why," he asks, "would anyone want to drink secretions from a cow's udder, or eat something that's popped out of a hen's butt?"

The conversation turns to the subject of Tibet. The country has been receiving a lot of publicity lately. *Seven Years in Tibet* has been turned into a successful movie and Martin Scorcese's *Kundun,* an artful biography of the Dalai Lama's early life, is currently showing at the Ojai Playhouse. Hollywood stars and other celebrities are becoming increasingly vocal in their support of the Dalai Lama. And Ojai has contributed, in its own modest way, with hundreds of "Free Tibet" signs stuck onto bumpers, front doors and even bicycles.

Mike visited Tibet in 1983, when the Chinese were allowing foreigners to enter the country for the first time since its occupation. The size of California, Utah, Arizona and Nevada combined, most of it above 15,000 feet, Tibet is the most mysterious place on earth and its people are arguably the most mystical.

Ojai and Tibet are linked in uncanny ways. The fictional utopia of Shangri-La was located in Tibet, and the Hollywood representation of it in the movie *Lost Horizon* was filmed in Ojai. Moreover, Krishnamurti, who lived much of his life in Ojai, was reputedly taught on the astral plane by materialized Tibetan masters Kuthumi and Lord Maitreya. The Master Kuthumi was reportedly more than five hundred years old and still living in a cave in the Himalayas, hidden in mountain fortresses in the forbidden kingdom.

Tibet and China are actors in a universal drama. Beneath the surface, unimaginable cosmic forces must be locked in an archetypal struggle. Tibet represents Spirit. Its atmosphere, if you don't respect it, is so rarefied it can kill you. When a Chinese basketball team from Shanghai visited Lhasa (elevation 11,830 feet above sea level), they blithely ignored medical advice and— having barely stepped off the plane—insisted on playing a fiercely competitive game. Two players died and the rest of the team had to be hospitalized and placed in oxygen tents.

Chinese intervention in Tibet represents the gross, material emotions of greed and envy. Its invasion of Tibet was in contempt of everything that is fine, lofty, sensitive, austerely beautiful and illuminated. Darkness attacked light and appeared to win.

However, the victory was perhaps only an appearance. The Dalai Lama leads his people in exile. He is the perfect incarnation of compassion and one of the great lights in human history. His presence on this planet is a blessing to us all. His struggle transcends Tibet and China; it is to do with good and evil, and it provides each of us with an opportunity to peer more deeply into goodness, to our eternal betterment. Even if the Dalai Lama were to lose the conflict at the literal level—and that story is far from over—he will have won on the level of planetary evolution.

Before leaving for Tibet, Mike asked a lama living in Ojai what gifts would be appropriate for the Tibetan people. Without hesitation, the monk replied that they prized a picture of His Holiness the Dalai Lama above all other earthly treasures. If some photos could be taken successfully through Chinese customs, that would be the greatest gift of all.

So Mike had two-hundred-and-fifty 8 inch by 10 inch glossies printed and he set off to Tibet with them. They were a source of delight wherever he went. Most of the monasteries had only one or two tiny, dog-eared black-and-white pictures of His Holiness pathetically displayed on the altar. To the monks, the Dalai Lama represented both political and spiritual freedom. His picture brought to them the one light shining in the dark night of genocide, oppression and cultural and environmental devastation. And it was particularly auspicious that a foreigner would come bearing this gift, since it meant that the outside world still remembered and still cared. Many tears were shed as, throughout the trip, the pictures touched Tibetan hearts.

In Tibet, Mike bumped into a crazy seeker, Ray, from Colorado. He'd brought a hang-glider with him and he was darned if he was going to leave Tibet without locating the whereabouts of the Master Kuthumi. He pictured himself sitting at the master's feet drinking in heady occult secrets known only to a handful of humans throughout history.

Ray's search had been unsuccessful up to that point, and he was taking a short break, as even the most ardent seekers must occasionally do. So Mike recruited him for a daring mission—to fly over remote regions of Tibet and scatter color photos to the monks and peasants, few of whom had ever seen a white man or a color photo, let alone a hang-glider.

The effect of all this craziness was to rekindle in the Tibetan people a renewed hope for freedom. Many of them realized for the first time that they were not alone, that the rest of the world was with them in spirit.

Shortly after his last mission, Ray finally located the cave where the Master Kuthumi was rumored to live. It was in a desolate hermitage on a wind-chilled mountainside near Shigatse. The cave was small and dark and eerie ... and completely empty. Ray found a monk and inquired about Kuthumi. The monk told him that the master had departed, but that he had left a note, which the monk handed to Ray. The note sounded like a practical joke, but Ray was unshakably convinced of its authenticity. It read: "Is too cold here. Lousy weather. Nothing to do. Left for Colorado. See you there. Master K."

Mike and Ray left Tibet three days later, and by that time the effect of their photo-dropping mission was reverberating around the country. Students were protesting in the streets and revolution was brewing among the Tibetan peasants. The virus of freedom was spreading. A Chinese crackdown ensued and Tibet was closed to tourism for over a year, striking testimony to the power of simple, nonviolent actions.

In such a way did Strength work its exquisite magic, as in these lines by Rilke:

Strength plays such a marvelous game—
It moves through the things of the world like a humble
servant,
groping out in roots, tapering in trunks,
and in the treetops like a rising from the dead.

Operating with wonderful creativity, patience and subtlety, the forces of good surfaced briefly and became visible. The pathways of an exiled lama in Ojai, a hip musician from Laurel Canyon and a guru-seeking hang-glider from Colorado intersected in time and space and images of the Dalai Lama rained down, in a shower of hope, on the beleaguered people of Tibet.

The Miracle of Strength is that it reveals the cosmic sense of humor. We have to be taking ourselves much too seriously, if we can look at the crumbling headstones of dead heroes and not chuckle. We are all going to die. And one day our planet will evaporate and disappear. From this perspective, our earnest displays of force, though they may have tragic consequences, are funny.

To experience true strength in action, we must let go of our ego, whose compulsion to control and manipulate life is an expression of fear and leads to suffering. As we surrender in this way, we will begin to see surface phenomena as a transparent veil beyond which we may commune with the Source. We realize that our fear-based lives are dreams from which we will eventually awaken.

We are like children playing a fierce game of tag; once we are called home, no trace of the game, or of our earnestness, will remain. Once home, there will be no place in heaven or on earth to point at and say, "There lie the remains of our illusions." The incoming tide of love will have washed them away.

If we can see, in a flash of insight, the absurdity of our violent postures, we will laugh—with relief, joy, amusement and gratitude.

"*There is no fear in love; but perfect love casteth out fear.*"

The New Testament

DEATH OF A HUSBAND
Courage

Courage is action from the heart, and thus it is inspired by love. Real courage is not showy or self-aggrandizing. Francesca, with her quiet fortitude in the face of adversity, demonstrates the miracle of courage.

FRANCESCA'S husband died nearly nine years ago. She was seven months pregnant with her daughter, Margaret. Her son, Alex, was five-and-a-half.

They had been living for eleven years in their "Mountain Home," a two-story wooden cabin in a remote wilderness area in Alpine County, Northern California. The nearest village was five miles away Three of these miles could only be covered on foot or on horseback. In winter, all five miles were inaccessible to motor vehicles.

Francesca's husband, Paul, hiked to the village and back every day in order to work. Once home, he would hoist Alex up onto his shoulders and take him off to chop wood, fix the water pipes, clean the pumps, clear the spring and generally keep busy until sunset.

He and Francesca had the earthy toughness that such an existence demanded. But, at the same time, they were sensitive people with a passionate interest in authentic spirituality and a touchingly sincere desire to understand the meaning of right livelihood and right relationship. No New Age bullshit for them. They went straight to the heart of the matter, with a directness and genuineness drawn from the rich, magnificent pine-clad land on which they lived.

I visited Francesca in Mountain Home—when she was there with her children on vacation—and I know and revere the place. One night, when the kids were in bed, we sat at the table by the wood-burning stove, drinking tea. She told me the story of her husband's death and we wept together. The tears were not for her particular story. They were stimulated by a sense of the vastness and the mystery of the universe, and the poignancy of the lives that we tiny human beings lead.

Today, Francesca and I are chatting in her home in Ojai. She has the complexion of an eighteen-year-old, but she's turning fifty next birthday She attributes her complexion to the one-day fast she does religiously every week. She says it helps clear the pores, and then laughs—a huge Alpine County laugh that comes up from her depths. I tell her that I think her skin's the way it is because she has the biggest, purest heart of anyone I know. And an ever-ready sense of humor. She laughs again.

I have such affection for this woman. She has an amazing heart, a wonderfully clear mind, nearly inexhaustible energy. She's so fair and honest and decent. She's lavished such love and attention on her Airedale that I know the dog will reincarnate as a human next time. There's an extraordinary intelligence and sensitivity in its eyes that's spooky.

"I wrote a poem about Paul in my creative writing class," she informs me shyly. "Would you like to hear it?"

I say I'd love to, and she recites it to me:

I do not wish for your return
And yet I miss you.
Tyrant of my life,
And greatest teacher.
I find you in my dreams
Where you are waiting,
And seeing your radiant face
Know that regret is folly.
Where are you now
With your fierce, imperious ways?

When I feel your presence,
There is only gentleness.

"It's beautiful," I tell her. "I think it shows you've finally healed."

"Yes, I think it does," she replies.

"Would you mind telling me the story of his death again?"

Francesca nods in agreement and, after taking a sip of mint tea, begins: "The first hint that there was anything different in his health was when we got back from Florida, where he'd been at a mathematics teachers convention and where Alex and I had been playing around and having a lovely time in Orlando. We got into our car and drove away from Reno Airport, with the Sierras on our right. Then, suddenly, Paul started to sneeze uncontrollably. He'd had hay fever before and there wasn't any real reason for alarm, but for some odd reason, I burst into tears. I turned to him and said, melodramatically, 'I'll always look after you.' I thought I was being silly, but really I had an unacknowledged premonition of doom.

"Over the next two months, we became concerned because these hay fever symptoms persisted, alternating with flu symptoms. Of course, being the way he was, he only took a day and a half off work and refused to go to the doctor. But in the end it became so severe that he asked me to talk to the local physician, Greg, about it, which I did, and Greg said he needed to be seen by a good internist. He said the only good one in the area was a woman, and he wondered if this would be a problem for Paul. I said to Greg that we women had been putting up with men examining us and prodding us for long enough, and that I thought Paul could damn well put up with a woman doing it to him for a while.

"The internist recommended tests at the hospital, which Paul, naturally, passed with flying colors—because that was the way he liked to do things. He got onto this exercise bicycle and impressed the hell out of all of them, and the doctor looked at him and said, 'You have the lungs of a twenty-one-year-old athlete.' I met him in the parking lot afterward and I remember he was triumphant about his performance, and I was very happy about the results too. I felt very light. I thought, 'Phew! He's in good shape. I don't have to worry.'

"I was pregnant with Margaret at the time, and the next day I stayed in the town to attend a Bradley child-birth clinic—all to do with letting go. Paul was supposed to have hiked back up to Mountain Home. In the middle of the class, there was a knock on the door and I heard Paul's voice. I thought, 'How nice—he's decided to come to class.' He hadn't come to many, and I remember thinking how supportive he was being. But it wasn't

99

that. He said he couldn't make it home. It was the worst he'd ever felt in his life, and the three-mile uphill hike back to our house was too much for him.

"We decided he wouldn't try going back up again. I said I'd run up and get some things and then we'd stay down in town. A group of friends accompanied Alex and me, because we couldn't bring enough belongings back on our own. Once the friends were loaded up, they left, and I set about the we're-leaving-for-a-while chores. After a while, I thought 'That's funny, I haven't heard from Paul.' We didn't have a phone, and so we communicated by radio. Normally, he would have called by then in order to check on us. I turned the radio on and shortly afterward I got a call from the deputy sheriff, Everett, informing me Paul had collapsed at the hot springs; he said I should come down. I asked if he was conscious when he was taken to hospital, and Everett replied that he didn't know. I said I'd pick up some things and come right down. And he said, 'No hurry'.

"That's when I knew. Little Alex was trotting along at my side, as we sped down the hill, and he picked up a stone and said, 'I'm going to give this to Daddy,' and I thought, 'No you're not.'

"Paul had been at the hot springs waiting for me to get back. Later, I got a very beautiful letter from a woman who had been there when he died. She spoke of the unity among everybody that day—how touching it was. How everybody was there for Paul in the most heartfelt way.

"A number of funny things happened—you look for signs at moments like this. As we were rushing down the mountain, a marvelous hawk came over my head. I noticed it and I knew it was there for me. And then I got to this lovely part of Pleasant Valley and a doe was standing there. She looked at me and I felt as if she were communicating with me—I felt her compassion, I think.

"Incidentally, something very odd happened exactly a year later, on the anniversary of Paul's death. I was going for a walk—just with little Margaret because Alex was at the library program—and I was in another part of Pleasant Valley when I saw a doe again. She didn't run away. She stayed with us for a while. In the eleven years I lived in that area, I had seen many does, but it was only on those two auspicious occasions that the creature seemed to approach me and want to comfort me. I sat down and cradled Margaret and cried; but the tears were for joy because I knew the deer's purpose was to reassure me.

"Anyway, we got down the mountain and headed straight for the sheriff's house. The corner house was owned by an old couple who were working in the garden

101

and they looked up at me. I waved, but they didn't wave back. They went back to their gardening. So then I knew the truth for sure. My best friend, Laura, came out and she said, 'I'm so sorry… but he didn't suffer.'

"We didn't know the cause of death immediately, but the autopsy showed that he'd died of blood clots in the lungs. The temperature of the hot springs had dislodged them.

"From Everett's we went to Laura's house. The District Nurse was there. She had been giving Laura all kinds of instructions on childbirth—in case the shock sent me into labor. Much later, Laura and I would laugh like crazy when we reminisced about the whole thing.

"Anyway, I sat in Laura's kitchen and cried for hours and hours. Then somebody brought me food, which surprised me. I thought, 'What are they doing bringing food at a time like this?' But they must have known me well, because I really enjoyed it. I remember thinking, 'Well, it hasn't put me off my victuals—that's a good sign!'

"When I'd finished eating and crying, I told everybody I was going back up the canyon. I said I wanted to go home. People asked why and Laura replied, 'Because Paul's there.'

"My friend, Peter, was in the house with us, and he and Laura accompanied Alex and me up the mountain. Alex still hadn't been told the news. He had been kept out in the garden while I was crying in Laura's kitchen. But I knew he took everything in because a few years later I overheard a conversation between him and a friend and I was surprised at how much he had understood.

"So, as we were walking up the mountain, I let Peter and Laura go ahead and I took Alex to one side to tell him what had happened. His little mouth opened. 'Who's going to take me skiing, hiking, snowmobiling?' he cried. I said, 'I don't know, but somebody will.' He said, 'When that baby comes out, it's going to want to know where its daddy is.' He was really concerned.

"He told me later that the reason he didn't cry very much at that time was because the hummingbirds had told him his daddy was going to die. There had been an enormous number around Laura's house that summer and he was riding his little bike like crazy all over the yard. Years afterward I learned that hummingbirds are messengers.

"Then we caught up with Peter and he carried Alex the rest of the way to Mountain Home.

"I went to bed upstairs, but I couldn't sleep, I was so full … of the news. I went outside to get wood for the stove, and it was the first time I had been alone. It was the first day of summer. It was a clear night and I looked up at the stars, and I just kept saying, 'Where are you? Where are you?'

103

"At dawn, I made this enormous breakfast for everybody. I don't know why but I had this great appetite in the middle of the heartbreak.'

"During the day, it was incredibly hot and Peter and Laura took Alex for a walk, while I made the necessary preparations to leave. Laura hadn't had time to bring a change of clothing; she was wearing a pair of jeans and was really boiling. So she took them off and started running around in this ten-year-old pair of raggedy knickers. It was a real scream.

"A few days after Paul's death, Alex was sitting in the bathtub, and he asked, 'Is it all a dream that Daddy was sick?' and I burst into tears and he said, 'It won't do for you to cry when we're sitting at the dinner table.' It was strange. He talked about some funny things. He said that when people die they lose their energy and you can take it, and I said, 'Yes I know,' because somehow I felt it too. He said, 'You know and you don't tell people. I know and I tell people.'

"That night we were taking a walk along this little road and there were all these shooting stars. Alex said they were his daddy. I mentioned the meteor shower to Laura, who's really up on these things. She told me that nothing had been predicted for that night.

"On another occasion, we were in Pleasant Valley and it was thundering and lightning along the ridge.

There was so much going on in the sky, and Alex said, 'Daddy's there. The fire in the hills is Daddy.' I gave him a hug and told him I'd been feeling the same thing, which I truly had.

"Another time, near the hot springs, we'd been hiking and suddenly I thought, 'Paul's right over there.' And just as I was thinking that, Alex said, 'Daddy's here.' We'd both get these things at the same time—it was weird.

"Paul loved Alex immensely. With him he had the opportunity to have the best relationship of his life. He didn't know there was anybody else in the universe until I came along, but with Alex he completely lost himself. He was about as ego-free as he could be. He had been this self-absorbed only child, but with Alex he opened up completely.

"Paul's principal quality was his strength and his persistence. I don't want this to sound New Age—because it was terribly serious—but ever since 1968 he was totally dedicated to spiritual inquiry, the quest for the Holy Grail. He was looking for the Holy Grail and he never stopped searching. He was a bastard in many ways, and would be the first to admit it, but there was this essence—it was the most important thing in his life, it really was.

"Our relationship wasn't easy, but I knew I could count on him totally—count on him to take care of things, to be

105

loyal, to fundamentally be there for me. He could absolutely hold it together, psychologically and physically.

"Also, we were wonderful teachers for each other. He taught me not to bring things up from the past. It was a fault I learned from my parents—in an argument, my dad would bring up minor things that had happened ten years previously as though they had just occurred and still stung him terribly. I thought it was the only way to fight. Paul broke me of the habit. He'd say, 'You can drop that—don't bring up the shit from the past.' And I knew he was right. Love makes no record of wrongs —I really started to understand that with him.

"Another thing was that I was so untidy by nature. During the last years of his life I was really trying to learn to not be a pig. Perhaps it was something in the brain! The other thing was being places on time. Those were the two big issues. They would make him furious. But I pointed out to him very clearly that this was going to affect Alex, if we carried on. So he stopped getting at me, and I tried as hard as I could to be neat and on time. The last three years were the most peaceful of the twenty we spent together.

"The week he died, he said beautiful things to me. I was so moved. He said I was graceful—don't laugh. I know it was an astonishing thing to say, but he said it. I was really touched.

"At first, after Paul's death, I thought I would have no money, but his boss got in touch with me and explained to me what I could expect. It wasn't much, but nevertheless I made a decision not to work—Paul would have had a fit if I had worked, with the baby.

"The day Margaret was born was the only day in seven months I didn't cry. It was so incredible; everything was so beautiful. Boy, I needed that day. I needed a lift.

"She was born in August and we stayed up in Mountain Home until the snows came. The day we left was Halloween night. Paul and I had been together twenty years and eleven of those had been spent in the canyon. I could scarcely register the fact that I was now packing up our stuff in order to leave this place and go and live God-knows-where and that Paul would never be here again with us. Alex, who had lived in the canyon his entire life—five-and-a-half years—spent the whole day on his bed.

"We used llamas to take our possessions down to the town. As they filed away from the clearing and headed down the narrow trail through the forest, I went down to the creek and I remember just shouting and shouting, over and over again, like a lunatic. I was in so much pain.

"Then I pulled myself together and left with the children. I had Margaret in a baby pack in front, a cat in one hand and Alex holding my other hand.

107

"There was a Halloween parade scheduled down in the town and Alex wanted to attend it dressed as a hiker; but by the time we got there it was over. I cried, thinking I'd let him down; however, firefighters and policemen and stores were still giving out candy, and Alex said that was all he really wanted and so it was OK for him.

"We spent the winter in a trailer. We slept on a leaking, moldy waterbed. The heater didn't work and so I used to turn the oven on and leave the door open in order to warm the place up. Then one day I got this strong feeling that I needed to stop doing that. The next day I tried to cook something and I discovered that the oven had suddenly developed a quirk—a little while after you lit it, it blew itself out and gas started to escape. I couldn't believe it. If I hadn't had that feeling that I should stop using the oven as a heater, the last thing I would have done the night before would have been to light the stove and go to bed. We would have been gassed.

"A similar thing happened one time in Mountain Home. We were asleep and there was a leak in the gas cylinder in the kitchen. I came down in the morning and saw the front door was wide open. I was really surprised, since—as you know—I'm particular about making sure the door's closed tight. It was quite mysterious. Then I smelled the gas, and it occurred to me that, without the open door, which was right next to the stove, we again probably would have been gassed.

"I'm sure we were being protected during that time —by Paul.

"There was another funny thing: when he died, I wanted very much to put a certain passage from Walt Whitman in the newspaper. It was a passage he loved. It has something to do with going to the edge, being a bold swimmer. It's so beautiful. I looked all the way through *Leaves of Grass* and other volumes of Whitman's poetry, but I couldn't find it. So I used another passage.

"Then, later, we were trying to get ready for a memorial service in Pleasant Valley; I took *Leaves of Grass* and I said, 'OK, Paul, if you're here show me the passage.' And I opened the book and there it was. At the time it surprised me very much. It was a library book—not as though the passage was dog-eared or anything.

"Throughout the winter, I was grieving terribly. There was a week of grace immediately after his death. A beautiful high—feeling the beauty of death, hearing music, seeing Paul in everything. I know that sounds weird. Every blade of grass was him. I got a glimpse of the fact that we are all one. It was a real stoned feeling. The only other time I've ever heard this was from somebody who attended Meher Baba's funeral in India. All she could say was 'Everything was him.'

"But the grief did come flooding in, and I started to feel enormously regretful that I hadn't said certain things to him before he died. I remember being really angry and screaming and crying—a lot of crying every day. One day, I thought, 'This has gone on long enough'—all the crying—and I decided to try and turn it off. Oddly enough, I received two letters that day. Both of them advised me not to stop crying. It was uncanny. So I did continue crying as much as I wanted, although after a while I stopped letting Alex see me. I know there's a phase of grieving in which you feel anger, but I never experienced it. I was glad Paul was released of his responsibilities. He had done well and been a super father. I remember fretting over money one day and saying to him, wherever he was, 'I'm really glad you don't have to do this anymore.'

"In a way, I felt a sense of the rightness of his death. He had to be in charge. He was a very strong type of man. He was the one who said what was what. But I was feeling ready to be the captain of my own ship. I didn't want anyone telling me what to do any more. So, I don't think he abandoned me by dying, although at one point I was seized with this horror that he had died because he didn't love me, because he didn't want to be with me any more. But then it hit me—I knew he would never do that. He would never leave Alex.

"So, I knew there had been love for me in his death. In a way, he had freed me.

"During the grieving process, we had many dreams. Alex had the first dream, and it was lovely. He and his daddy were sitting opposite each other. And Alex said to Paul, 'This doesn't seem like a dream.' And Paul said, 'So it isn't.' And that was it. Alex told me the dream and I cried, thinking: 'I'll never get a dream.' But I did.

It was July 19th, less than a month after he had died, and there he was in my dream. 'Don't you know,' he said, in his strict voice—'Don't you know that I'm always here when you need me?' I said, 'Well I seem to feel that you are.' And he said, in his for-God's-sake-woman tone, but in a loving way too, 'Of course, I am.' I woke up immediately and I had a shower and I felt fabulous the whole day. A shift occurred in me that night. Months later, I talked about it with my friend Laura and she said she had seen it, though she never said anything to me.

"And then I had a dream of his—it's a lovely word —transfiguration. You know, your face becomes radiant. I dreamed I was at Mountain Home and I felt an arm leading me down the steps, and I put my head on his shoulder, and I said all the things I wished I'd been as a wife—I wished I'd been this, that and the other, and all the regrets came pouring out. Then it occurred to me that I was going to be allowed to look at him. I turned and gazed at his face. It was his face, but very radiant, very different. It was so odd—all human care had been dropped. All my apologetic, silly regrets were clearly ridiculous. I had to let go of them. He said, 'They're so good to me,' and then added, 'You're the ones who are dead.' And that was it.

"The final dream was seven months later, when I stopped grieving. It was a release—we released each other telepathically. And I said, 'Is it all right?' I think I had in mind, 'Is it all right that I love someone else?' When I woke up I thought, 'I won't dream about him again. It's over now.' And it was."

It's several weeks since we spoke and I am sitting in Mountain Home. I have come here for a few days to relax and to edit my book.

It is June, the sky is a clear blue and the creek —which snakes around the hill upon which the house is perched—is rushing, swollen by the exceptional El Niño rains that, until recently, have been pounding the surrounding mountain tops.

There is not a single human sound. Flies buzz around the deck, en route for piles of dung left by bears, coyotes and deer. Butterflies float past on the breeze, their fluttering yellow wings keeping them aloft, but not apparently controlling their direction. Blue jays chatter in the pine trees, looking bossy and important. The dense forest waits patiently at the edge of the clearing, ready to slowly take over should the human presence here cease definitively.

I am alone. It is the first time I have been here without company, and it's delicious. I can feel my cares drop away and life in Ojai become a misty memory. I feel I could live here for eleven years, as Francesca did, and be perfectly happy. But two divorces and three children living on different continents make this impractical. I look around the house—it truly is a home. There are not a lot of ornaments, but everything is expressive of Paul and Francesca. He loved to read Carlos Castaneda, Krishnamurti and Gurdjieff, and there is an extensive collection of their works on the bookshelves. Francesca met and admires Joseph Chilton Pearce, and *Magical Child* and a few of his other works are dotted around the shelves.

There are paintings on the walls of idyllic pastoral landscapes. A gigantic copy of Rudyard Kipling's poem, *If,* is hung in a frame on the wall. In the kitchen, a well-crafted rack, made by Francesca's father, is home to whisks, knives, ladles, can openers and every other utensil.

The house is representative of an era of Francesca's life, one that is inseparable from Paul. I am sure it was he who hung *If* on the wall. And down by the creek in a makeshift shed—miraculously just about standing after nine winters have battered it—there are broken solar panels, industrial batteries, wires, a fridge and other comfort-making pieces of technology that nobody since his death has had the skill or inclination to resuscitate.

I prepare myself a bowl of rice and vegetables and eat it at the dining-room table. Kahlil Gibran's masterpiece *The Prophet* catches my eye, half visible between *The Education of Little Tree* and *Winnie-the-Pooh.* I take the book out of the shelf and open it. It is inscribed: "3/8/69 To Francesca, to read in quiet moments. Mrs. York." The book must have been a gift from her mother-in-law, probably in the early days of her relationship with Paul. The wording of the inscription is strangely formal.

There is a folded sheet of paper inside the cover. On the back there is a pen and ink drawing of morning glories. I unfold the paper and my eyes fall on the heading: "Paul Stanley York, 11 October 1944—22 June 1989." It is the program for Paul's memorial service.

Come the morning I'll be far from here
Slowly rising in another sphere

Home, world good-bye 'cause I'll be home
In the sky in the morning, bye bye … bye bye.

The program lists various prayers and recitations, including ones from *Leaves of Grass* and *The Prophet*. It indicates that the service is to be held in Pleasant Valley Meadow.

A shiver comes over me. I recall that I have been noticing Paul and thinking about him all morning. His presence has caught my attention on numerous occasions. I wonder what the date is today, I've lost track. I count on my fingers from June 17th, when I arrived, and calculate that today is the 22nd—the anniversary of Paul's death.

I wonder what section they chose from *The Prophet*. The program doesn't say. The passage on love floats into my mind and, as I thumb through the pages looking for it, the book fall's open at the correct page. It has been marked by a small, black-and-white photo of Francesca. She looks about ten and she's standing in front of an austere building, dressed in her schoolgirl uniform.

A few lines of the text catch my eye:

When love beckons to you, follow him,
Though his ways are hard and steep.

115

And when his wings enfold you yield to him,
Though his sword hidden among his
Pinions may wound you.
And when he speaks to you believe in him
Though his voice may shatter your dreams
As the north wind lays waste the garden.

I close the book and replace it on the shelf. It is dusk and so I light one of Francesca's hurricane lamps. Sitting in an easy chair, I dreamily watch the dancing shadows projected onto the walls by the sputtering lamp. In a few weeks, Francesca will be up here with her children for the school vacation. At the end of the summer, it will be her fiftieth birthday. She will be celebrating simply in the lush green meadow in Pleasant Valley, joined by a handful of her closest friends. A few days later, she and her children will be driven to San Francisco to fly off on a two-year trip to Europe and India. There is no certainty that, at the end of two years, she will, return to California. I feel sad at the thought of this.

An era has ended for Francesca and a new one has begun. Her relationship with Paul and her period of mourning—together spanning nearly her whole adult life—are over. Soon she will be leaving it all behind her, both physically and emotionally, and boarding a plane that will take her and her children into a totally new world.

Francesca admits that the prospect of living in India with two children terrifies her. But it's something she knows she must do. Love has beckoned to her and, with characteristic courage and faith, she will follow.

The Miracle of Courage is that it connects us with the source of all love. It is the antidote to fear. Francesca could not have survived her experiences without it. And yet it was not a weapon that she unsheathed when needed; it was an integral part of her nature.

Courage strengthens our qualities and reveals them to us. It molds and shapes us. If we are serious about taking the path of our highest good, we will constantly meet monsters whose mission is to scare us away from our purpose. Sticking to our path, or even simply seeing where it is, while being guided by only the faintest of lights or the softest of whispers, requires unflagging courage and determination.

It takes courage to follow our dreams, when to do so seems crazy; to be alive when there's nothing left to live for; to remain alone, when a relationship will not serve us; to feel love in the midst of rage; to stay true while wracked with fear. It takes courage to choose to heal rather than to die.

Beyond courage, however, there is the vision of a life free of fear, where the monsters are seen for what they are: mirages with no substance. Then courage will become a strange and wonderful exhibit in the museum of life, and we will live in spontaneous right action.

"Sell your cleverness and buy bewilderment; cleverness is mere opinion, bewilderment is intuition."

Rumi

9

DEATH OF A WIFE
Acceptance

My conversation with Tim was funny and frustrating all at the same time. Reflecting on it later, I understood that I'd been trying to fit him into a spiritual mold, and he would have none of it. Superficially, I'd given him space to express himself, but in my heart I hadn't been receptive to what he had to say. I'd brought my cleverness—my knowledge—into the discussion, and the result was a climate of insensitivity and intolerance. After our conversation, too late to change anything, I appreciated the power of acceptance.

TIM WAS born six days after me in the same city —Liverpool, England. We both left England in our early twenties and, after extensive travels, ended up in the same tiny town perched on the western edge of the United States.

"So what?" I imagine Tim saying. "When will people stop trying to make something out of nothing? We live in an infinite universe where anything is possible. Karmic connections are possible. Coincidences are possible. I can't know. And, quite honestly, I don't care. All we've got is the now. Right now, we're both sitting here in a coffee shop in Ojai, and that's all there is."

His wife, Amanda, died three years ago. Tim is a tough realist, who tries valiantly to remain ensconced in the "now," but he is still grieving the loss.

Amanda and he were married less than a year after they met. "We were soul mates," Tim says. He realizes he's let slip an esoteric term and backs off a little: "It was just a desire for both of us to be in the same place at the same time." Then, in an exasperated tone—I'm uncertain whether it's directed at himself or at me—he adds: "We ascribe metaphysical reasons to some quite practical things. It just was.

"We lived in Los Angeles for most of our marriage, but in 1994 I sold my business and we moved to Ojai. We both wanted a change, and we wanted the children to be in the country. We moved into this house in the East End and three months later Amanda started complaining of breathing difficulties. She saw a lung specialist and found out she had fluid build-up in the pleural cavity, which is a sign of a gynaeco-logical cancer. Two days later it was confirmed—she had ovarian cancer. I knew the moment I heard the news that she was going to die. Intuitively I knew this was the end of her life and of my life.

"Initially, we both withdrew from each other—for me it was a survival mechanism—but we reconnected when, nineteen months later, she went through the actual death process.

"I watched Amanda die and I started to question all my old behavior. I realized we only have one life to lead. We can't live in the future. We can't live in the 'what-might-be.' When my wife closed her eyes finally at one o'clock in the morning on Saturday, November 16th—that was it. There was no more 'We'll go to the beach tomorrow' or 'We'll play with the kids on Sunday.' That's when it hit me: a life lived for the future is wasted.

"I also saw the futility of negative feelings. I used to always look at the glass as half empty."

"And now you see it as half full?" I offer, eagerly exhibiting attentiveness.

"No, now I see it as just a glass."

"So, now you're content?"

"No, I'm not content; but I'm happy. Discontent drives me. Happiness is a being situation. I can be very discontent, but happy."

"Did you have any religious or spiritual experience at the time of your wife's death?" I ask hopefully.

"In my childhood I was extremely religious—orthodox Jewish—and one day I woke up and realized it was

123

a bunch of crap. I've been an atheist and I've been an agnostic."

"And what do you believe now?"

"I do have a belief, born out of logic, born out of the nature of physical reality. If we live in an infinite universe, then anything is possible. Without limitation you can have anything. You can have a god. You can not have a god. The question is, 'Does it matter?'"

"Does it matter?"

"No, it doesn't. But the question you should really be asking me is: 'Do I have faith?'"

"Do you have faith?" I ask weakly.

"No, I don't! I have faith in the trivial sense—the sun will rise tomorrow, and so on. But do I have faith in an externality? No, absolutely not. I can't accept things that I cannot touch. I don't believe in an external god. Sure, there are higher forces in the universe—but so what? There are lower forces too. Are you talking about humanity? We're just a species of animal that happens to have more reasoning powers than a lower species of animal. And as such—so what?

"To me, all that matters is the Golden Rule—'Do unto others as you would have them do unto you.' That's all. Everything else is commentary."

"So you don't believe," I ask, "in a soul-identity that continues after death?"

"Amanda was convinced she would go to a planet where she could do art forever. As for me, I believe in reincarnation, but on the atomic level. Everything gets re-constituted into something else. You've got a battery and it's discharged—where did the life force go? It got used up. When the life is over and you've got no more energy in it, you recycle the battery case. The energy used is still out there; it's just in a different, unknowable form."

"How do you feel, knowing that she's been reab-sorbed into the cosmos, and thus has been basically extinguished?"

"I'm OK with it. Plato had a great expression—it's not men who are immortal, it's their ideas. She lives for me in some way, but I don't want to anthropomorphize it. It's the memories that live, the ideas that live, her works that live. Her survival as an individual still doesn't fit my para-digm. Even if her energy is flowing around somewhere it's not a unified whole. It might be reconstituted into another form, and because the universe is infinite it might be reconstituted as her. I'm not unwilling to accept the possibility. It's irrelevant whether I believe in it or not, whether it's true or not. I'm just this little speck with this whole fucking universe out there; I can't know everything in my universe, it's not possible. In an infinite universe it's quite possible that she could walk into this coffee shop right now—and frankly I dream about her the whole time

125

as though she's doing that very thing—but it's so far removed from my sphere of reference."

"Would you say then," I suggest, hopeful that the Zen approach will get us back on reassuring ground, "that you have a healthy respect for an 'I-don't-know' attitude?"

"No. It's not that I don't know; it's that I can't know. I can't know everything. The corollary is I can know some things."

"The implication being," I suggest, "that you can't possibly know the answers to the fundamental questions about life. That seems like an enormous thing to be certain about."

"What do you mean by the fundamental questions about life?" Tim asks with rising exasperation. "Where we came from? Where we're going?—I don't give a shit. Watching somebody die for no apparent reason —forty-four-year-old women whom you love are not supposed to die—brings you to the only place you can come to, which is accepting it. It happened. I don't know why. I'll never know why. It just happened. I have an engineering background, so I look at things as con-structs—How is it made? Why is it broken? How can I fix it? But for this kind of thing you can't fix it. It just is."

I can feel myself getting judgmental, and so I look for the quality in Tim that lies behind his peculiar sense of certainty. It doesn't take long to find it. "The way you approach life," I observe, "strikes me as having great qualities. You are somebody who wants to be honest and you don't want to bullshit yourself or have other people be that way. I see, and have respect for, what energizes this attitude in you. It comes from a good place, I know."

I see his eyes soften, and I feel that we're finally making contact. However, I can't resist continuing with a "but," and the connection is lost again.

"But," I continue, "don't you find that your understanding of life progressively deepens? Take jealousy as an example: at a primitive level we think that the other person's actions are actually causing us hurt, and we blame him or her for them. Then, for whatever reason, we go down into a deeper level of principle, into a deeper level of understanding …"

"Let me shorten this for you," Tim interjects impatiently "You own your own feelings."

"Yes, and when you do, there's a deeper level of understanding about the way things are. Shouldn't we at least be open to the possibility of understanding what our lives and the universe are all about?"

"How could I be so bold as to presume to know what the universe is about? It isn't about anything, it just is. Why can't you get off this mumbo-jumbo about there being deeper meanings to things?"

127

"I'm just advocating the 'I-don't-know' position, an openness to possibilities."

"What you don't understand is that I don't fucking care. It makes not one whit to me whether there's God there or God everywhere or God anywhere else. You know something, there's no practical effect for me. I'm still going to live my life as a good person. I follow the Golden Rule. So, if I'm going to be an asshole I would expect someone to be an asshole back to me.

"Ultimately, if you truly attempt to live in the moment (I think it's an attempt, it's work, because we're programmed by society not to live in the present), if you truly live in the moment, what difference does it all make? You're only experiencing the now; and if the now happens to be reading, or having this kind of conversation, or drinking tea, or whatever, that's all we are. We're not anything else than this present moment. We are the sum total of everything that happened up to this present moment. And only that much. We haven't got the cure for cancer—it hasn't happened yet. We can think about it, we can theorize about it, but the moment is what's important. Watching somebody die in front of your eyes makes you realize that the only time you have is that moment—you don't have a tomorrow."

"So how do you occupy the succession of 'now' moments?" I ask.

"The question contains a contradiction," Tim replies. "You don't occupy a 'now moment' with things; it's the process itself which fills the moment. Whatever is unfolding in the now is what you occupy yourself with."

"Which means," I suggest, "that you could be thinking of the past or the future and still be in the now."

"Yes, you could be reflecting on the Napoleonic wars and be in the 'now,' but not necessarily. You could even be worried about something and still be present in the now."

"Do you ever worry?" I ask him, hoping he'll expose his vulnerability.

"Don't be ridiculous!" he exclaims. "Of course, I worry. I'm subject to the same emotional forces that you are."

"What do you worry about?"

"I worry about my trees. I have to learn about trees in order to prevent them from doing things I don't want them to do. Like fall down. I don't worry about things I have no control over—groundhogs, snails and other forces of life that go on their own inexorable path. It's kind of a fun thing to worry about. Worry's the wrong word—it's fun to not know what the trees are going to do. You just surrender to it."

Tim picks up his *Wall Street Journal,* which is his signal that he feels he's said all he can or needs to say.

129

Later, we say our good-byes and he leaves the coffeehouse. As I watch the glass door swing shut behind him, I think how much good it would do him to cry his heart out nonstop for a whole weekend. But then I remember something he told me once: "I can't stand whiners. I can't stand people who look at life and get stuck. I've been stuck, I've been to therapists, but in the end you just have to get on with it—without looking for Big Daddy."

An intense melancholy descends on me. Perhaps he's right. Maybe we are all fooling ourselves that something magnificent is just around the corner. Maybe, as Marty Van Loan sings on the *Left of Memphis* CD, "... our quests for freedom are cages in disguise."

I feel disgruntled. I wonder why, and then the truth dawns on me. Many of Tim's views on life clash with mine, and I have been resistant to them. I have a lesson to learn—the lesson of unconditional acceptance—not in the sense of believing everything a person says, but as a total openness that allows a person to be exactly who he is. Then there is compassion, and where there is compassion there is true communication.

The Miracle of Acceptance is that it makes every problem in life vanish. Acceptance involves allowing the present moment to be exactly what it is, without judging it. When we do this, we experience abiding peace.

Does this imply that we should passively allow everything and anything? No, of course not. We still take action, but we flow with the present moment, without resisting it.

When we accept life, we accept other people. This means honoring the fact that their lives are unfolding mysteriously according to a divine plan. We draw individuals into our lives who mirror us perfectly—that is part of the divine plan. From this perspective, a person is never a problem, but a messenger who can tell us something we need to know about ourselves.

We cannot give to others what we have not first given to ourselves, and so, to accept others and to accept life, we must start with self-acceptance. Since we have received such heavy self-rejection programming, this is a Herculean task. But it is not impossible to learn to accept what we have been denying and repressing all our lives. When we do this, our disowned selves are brought into the Light, where they are bathed in an ocean of love and effortlessly transformed.

"*If you are not the person you think you are, you have none of the problems you think you have.*"

Vernon Howard

DEATH OF A SON
Non-Attachment

Fortified by a special connection with the Indian mystic, Sai Baba, Stan learns the wisdom of non-attachment: if we're not attached to any specific outcome in Life, including even the survival of our child, we are brought fully into the now. And then our understanding of who we are and what is happening to us is transformed.

STAN HAS just returned from India. He went there to go hiking in the Himalayas. He expected to stay there a couple of months and return as he had left—alone —but he stayed three years and came back with an angelically sweet German fiancée, Christina.

Stan has a neat, trim appearance. He drinks a small coffee in a trim, white cup, instead of the purple or pink bowl-like cups in which the regular size is served. The word "efficiency" comes to mind when you meet him. He looks efficient and he speaks efficiently. He has a

133

quiet, soothing voice, with a tone that implies: "It's not a big deal—nothing's a big deal. Everything's just the way it is."

I can feel myself getting suspicious. My initial reaction is to disbelieve somebody who says nothing's a big deal. Perhaps it's because I have so much emotion bubbling inside me I assume that everybody else does too, and that if they don't reveal it they're just repressing and denying it.

While in India, he explains to me, he went down to Goa, a decadent resort area favored by Westerners, and ran into Christina there. I ask him if he had a sense of Destiny looking him in the eyes and saying, "Go for it, Stan, this is the one."

Stan replies, "There are no coincidences," in a matter-of-fact voice that doesn't seem to me to do justice to the fact that we're alluding to the miraculous —a Master Conductor, orchestrating all our experiences in perfect synchrony for an unimaginable good.

He adds simply, "She was just a beautiful lady, sitting on a beach and I said to myself, 'Get away from this.' But, I didn't!

"In Goa, Christina spoke to me about the famous Indian guru, Sai Baba—all the good things he had done; how he didn't ask for money and wasn't a phony claiming all sorts of things and doing nothing.

"Although I was interested in spirituality at that time, I had never been particularly drawn to organized religion. I had heard teachers speak, read various self-help books and been to workshops, but nothing truly resonated with me. I preferred to be by myself in nature and find spiritual meaning there.

"But then one day, as I was walking along the beach in Goa, I was suddenly filled with bliss and this vision came to me, an image of Sai Baba telling me to go to the ashram. Light was pouring out of my fingers." He takes a sip of coffee. "It was intense," he adds, without any intensity.

"I told Christina about it and said I wanted to go there. She was concerned I wouldn't like it. 'The men just sit on the floor all day and do nothing,' she said. And she was right. It was two years before Sai Baba spoke to me. But the important thing is not getting an interview, it's just being there. Who am I to judge when the appropriate moment is for an interview? In his presence something is happening to you all the time."

I am incredulous. "Surely," I insist, "two years without talking to the Master must have been frustrating."

"Were there moments," Stan replies, "of wondering what I was doing there? Absolutely. But I soon realized that he was an avatar—a being who, of his own will, decided to come down to earth to show us a way

135

of life and help the world. How do I know that? I really don't know anything and it really doesn't matter. What matters is what is happening inside of me.

"Of course," he continues, as though speaking of the least fabulous stories ever told, "there are fabulous stories—for example, his appearance on the other side of the planet while talking to somebody in the ashram. You can believe it or not, it really doesn't matter. I do —I just know. One time Sai Baba materialized a Rolex watch in the ashram, complete with the date of purchase (the same date as the materialization) and the place of purchase—New York City. Later, the person who received it went to the store in New York and checked up on it. When he gave the date to the sales assistant, she remembered the purchase perfectly— who could forget a strange-looking man, with a big Afro, wearing an orange robe?"

I ask him to tell me about his interview with Sai Baba.

"About ten of us walked into this small room, with a tiny doorway, and then on into a private room in back of that. Immediately, I was just filled with his presence. He materialized vibhuti, sacred ash, and gave it to the women. Sai Baba says that he materializes vibhuti to those who come to him with love and devotion. It symbolizes the life-and-death cycle in which everything ultimately turns back to dust. It is a reminder to give up desires, passions and temptations. It has healing properties and can cure illnesses—I know of several miraculous cases.

"Later, he materialized a ring for me—I saw it appear out of his hand. A cynic might claim a magician can do that, and of course he can. But I've seen him take a ring, blow on it, and change it from silver to gold. I was right close up."

"What did you talk about?" I asked.

"We talked about my son. But what he says to you is not the important part of being with him. He has an incredibly high vibration that raises your own. You feel yourself being transformed in his presence. It's not to do with the words."

A sadness came into Stan's eyes when he mentioned his son, and so I ask for details.

"He had died a few months before," Stan tells me. "One morning I was sitting in the main room and Sai Baba, as was his custom, walked through. For the first time since I'd been there, he came over to me. He looked me in the eyes with indescribable compassion and love. A week later I got the phone call every parent dreads—my son had died of a drug overdose. It had happened on the same day Sai Baba walked over and looked at me. I hadn't got the news immediately

137

because my ex-wife was away at the time and nobody knew how to contact me.

"During the interview Sai Baba told me my son was OK, and I believed him, even though I was feeling intense grief.

"I still worry about my son to this day. A part of me misses him very much. I grieve and cry for him. It's been very sad and difficult. I pray for him and wish him well.

"But fatherhood is not a possessive thing. In a wonderful way, Sai Baba helped me understand this. You can write letters to him and he responds to them. I wrote a series of letters before my son's death and, under Sai Baba's invisible guidance, I went from writing 'my son' to writing 'our son' and then 'His son.' I began to understand that my son is a child of God. We're all God's children. And we are loved in ways that we cannot fathom. Death is only a passing. We look at it one way—a catastrophe—but it's just our soul's journey.

"When I got the news, I returned to California for a while. I went to my home in Santa Monica, but once I was there, I was told intuitively to go to Ojai. Christina and I stayed in a teepee at the Ojai Foundation. It's a healing spot, and we met a lady there whose son had died in a similar situation eight years before. We were able to share that, and it was very helpful. We went on a vision quest and we did some counseling. Basically, though, just being in nature and working outside helped me deal with my grief.

"His death has affected my life in a number of subtle ways, good and bad. But the bottom line is—it just is. Life is not about any past event; life is just being here now. When I screw up it's because I'm dwelling in the past or projecting into the future. The secret to enlightenment is to live in the now. That's all."

"What was your son's name?" I ask.

"Trevor," Stan says. He looks at me intently. "Why are we talking about this?"

"I'm interested," I explain, "in how your exposure to Sai Baba influenced your experience of what, for many of us, would be the worst event that could happen in our lives. We want spiritual teachings, I assume, to translate into less suffering and more joy."

"God's grace," Stan says, "operates at an entirely different level. The spiritual path is not to do with lessening suffering—it's to do with losing your ego, and that's painful. Having said that, after three years with Sai Baba, I do experience life differently. Do I get frustrated? Sometimes. Do I get upset? Sometimes. But not as much as before.

"*All* our negative experiences originate in fear. What is fear?—lack of faith in the perfection of the moment. And so we leave the now and go roaming about in the past and the future; but there's no safety in either of those two places. There's nothing for us to think about or figure out. Things just are, that's all."

"It seems," I say, "that you stick very close to what you actually, truly know—most people don't. They go off into opinion and speculation."

"Yes. The trick is to see things as they are—to realize that our belief is different than our knowledge, our fantasy different than our experience. I believe we're all capable of being enlightened and seeing life from a totally different perspective. The key is not to be attached to our conditioned expectations of how events should be. It is the attachment to our desired outcomes that leads us down a path of suffering."

I believe that too. And I believe in Stan and what he's learned. I've warmed to him and think he's a fine emissary for Sai Baba. There's something solid and reliable about him—what you see, albeit lacking in pizzazz, is what you get. In a world filled with spiritual hyperbole, his low-key, somewhat monotonous account of his experiences is oddly reassuring. I realize that it doesn't matter whether or not you deliver your lines with the passion of Sir Lawrence Olivier. It's the inner experience that counts, and authentic understanding doesn't need theatrical accompaniment. If it's genuine, it ultimately reveals itself—without drama.

We part company and I return home. I sense there's a lesson for me in our conversation. And so, closing my eyes and asking for guidance, I intuitively take a book from my bookshelf and open it at random. I come across a passage from Schopenhauer:

If you want your judgment to be accepted, express it coolly and without passion. All violence has its origin in the will, and so, if your judgment is expressed with vehemence, people will consider it an effort of will, and not the outcome of knowledge, which in its nature is calm and unemotional.

"Wow!" I exclaim out loud. "That's Stan to a 'T'!" I realize I am being neither cool nor dispassionate. Invisible forces have guided me to a perfectly apposite text which answers my question, and that makes me feel effusive and amazed. "I know there's an unseen order," I vehemently tell an imaginary Schopenhauer, "and matter-of-factness is not adequate—only wonderment will do."

The Miracle of Non-Attachment is that it's the secret to living joyfully, regardless of circumstances. If we believe in the reality of sickness and death, we might find it difficult to accept this. But non-attachment leads us into the heart of Life's mystery and shows us that death is an illusion. Not that we will suddenly face everything with equanimity. Stan naturally felt grief over his son's death; but he used the suffering to penetrate more deeply into the truth of things.

If we examine our lives honestly, we'll observe that attachment is not a wise psychological state. Indeed, it is the source of all our suffering. We have been attached to cars, pets, lovers, success, failure, spousal cooperation and unencumbered freeways. When reality has met our expectations, we have been happy; when it has not, we have been pained.

We need to peer into the vicissitudes of life's events and seek the imperturbable, constant truth that lies beneath them. We are like a child who has discovered two jewels; one a shiny glass bead of little real value, the other an uncut diamond encrusted with rock. We need to see that all our attachments are to glass beads. When life tugs on these beads, we appear to suffer; and yet, in a spirit of immense caring, an opportunity is being offered to us—an opportunity to uncover the authentic jewel, the one that is beyond price.

"The desire for intimacy is the longing to reconnect with the Self."

A.H. Almaas

MOMENT OF RECOGNITION
Intimacy

We are strange creatures, and we seek out connections with one another in strange ways. But who is to say what is right and wrong? Perhaps, acting from hidden impulses of the soul, we always create the circumstances we need in order to grow. In this story, the mystery of intimacy is examined.

IT IS THE month of May and Nick has flown in from England for the day; it's his son's eighteenth birthday and he wants to be here for it. He flew with Virgin, seated at the Upper Class bar drinking cognac with members of the rock band Def Leppard. They each drank a whole bottle. Nick looks the part: with long, expensively styled hair, wearing a hand-tailored black linen jacket and old, faded jeans, he has the insouciance of an aging British rock star. Unless you're one of the cognoscenti, you wonder if he is that guitarist with the Rolling Stones —the one who replaced Mick Taylor. In fact, he is an advertising whiz who jets around the world first-class on behalf of one of the biggest agencies, his mission to

145

ensure that the company's distant outposts remain strong and profitable. He completes this mission with dedication and nearly total success, and he is paid a fortune in return.

Within fifteen minutes of arriving at Los Angeles he is heading for Ojai in a rented car, drunk and driving ninety-five miles an hour.

He arrives in Ojai to discover that his son has plans — adults are banished from the house for the night; the teenagers are partying on their own. Nick has until seven o'clock, and then he and his soon-to-be ex-wife, Marianne, are to go to separate rooms at the Inn. To the dismay of his sons, he spends the time until then drinking Carlo Rossi burgundy from a gallon carafe, interspersed with periodic naps taken spread-eagled on the living-room floor.

At 8:00 P.M. Nick and Marianne go to the Calypso Bar and Grill to have dinner and, in Nick's case, to drink a lot of gin and tonic. "Just rinse the glass out with tonic," he explains to the bemused waitress, "and then fill the glass up with gin." He has an English accent, oodles of charm and evidently loads of money. She's been a waitress long enough to know the unspoken agreement: "Bring me everything I ask for without demur, whether or not it's on your menu, and in return I'll pay whatever you want for it…. Oh, and the tip will be large."

William joins them for dinner. He and Nick became friends as fellow trainees in an advertising agency twenty-five years ago. At the time, Nick and Marianne were living together. As Marianne has progressively shifted her attention from money, home, family and basic Catholic values to an eclectic investigation of matters of physical, mental and spiritual health, she and William have become closer. He left advertising after a year and discovered a passion for the same subjects as Marianne. They have a platonic, but very intimate, friendship.

Marianne's relationship with her husband, however, has become more distant. Two years ago, she decided she had come to the end of the line with him. He was unremittingly contemptuous about her forays into astrology, aromatherapy, massage, Reiki, tarot, psycho-therapy and metaphysics. He also scoffed at her plan to create a chain of aromatherapy stores and healing centers. She felt they had nothing in common anymore.

She also decided that she'd had enough of England —its poor climate, its petty-mindedness, its danger. In the city of Brighton, where they lived, there was no sense of safety. The crime rate was appalling—they had been burglarized twice—and there was a hefty sprinkling of "bad" kids mixed in with the good ones her boys hung out with.

147

Marianne enrolled the boys in Oak Grove School and moved to Ojai. Her reasons for the move were compelling—a nurturing school, a safe town, a sunny climate, spiritually-inclined inhabitants and, above all, seven thousand miles of land and ocean between her and her husband and parents.

Nick and Marianne are engaged in a heated conversation when William enters the restaurant. He observes their sparring interactions with amusement. The change in Marianne's personality never ceases to astonish him. She used to be so retiring and unassertive that she would often go through an entire evening scarcely saying a word. But that has changed. Her studies and her therapy sessions have brought her into her own power, much to the consternation of her husband and her parents, none of whom have any desire to see the compliant, simple Marianne they all know turn into a self motivated person, with ideas of her own, many of them occult and disturbingly bizarre.

To see the three of them now, drinking in the Calypso Bar, no one would suspect there was so much sub-text. Through the miracle of repression and denial, the evening continues as if everything were in order.

However, there is something different tonight. Nick is more emotional than usual. It's the first time he's visited

148

Ojai since his mother died a few months ago. Outwardly, he professes to have hated her all his life; yet, during her final months, he spent more time with her and cared for her more than either his brother or sister did. He has clearly been devastated by her death. The man who is master of the business world, in which he spends most of his time, crumbled on the day his mother died. He was on the phone to his family in Ojai in tears. Marianne, who has a soft spot for Nick and always will, sent their older son on the next plane to England to be with his father and give him support.

"William," Nick suddenly exclaims with a slight slur, "you and I are the same. Neither of us could speak until we were four—me because, as a toddler, I was run over by a tractor; you because you were born defective."

"I did speak," William retorted, "but just not a language that anybody other than my sister understood."

Heedless of William's protest, Nick continues: "And we've both lost a parent. We both know how that feels."

William is astounded. As incredible as it may seem to normal, candid, communicative people—if they truly exist—this conversation is the nearest William and Nick have got to intimacy in twenty-five years, and it can't all be attributed to the liquor.

149

"You know," Nick adds, "We look at life in the same way too. We both know it's shit. We both know everybody's a phony. We just react in different ways. Seeing through the system, I know how to make it work for me—and I do. Seeing through the system, you disappear off into remote mountain valleys and go cosmic."

There's truth in this. Having both started their careers in advertising, and seen the phoniness of the whole business, they reacted in opposite ways—Nick used his insight to play the game and make a fortune; William immersed himself in fascinating, but impractical metaphysical pursuits.

Nick leans over and whispers across the table: "You're like the other half of me. And the worst part is, I feel I can only keep my role—'successful executive'—for as long as you keep yours, 'failed metaphysician.' If you ever make a fortune, everything I've got would come tumbling down. That's why everything's fine as long as I'm always paying the check for you, which so far I always am. I keep a close eye on you, William."

This is about as near to the bone as it's going to get tonight, and it's time to find a distraction. William suggests champagne and Nick orders it.

They leave in the early hours of the morning, having played darts and pool for the rest of the night. Nick walks back to the hotel and Marianne drives William home. Before she does so, however, she drives up the Denison Grade, the pass connecting the upper and lower valleys, and she and William sit at the viewpoint for a few hours soaking in the beautiful night and talking drunkenly of this and that.

Nick makes no mention of the strange hours Marianne has been keeping. He cares for her; there can be no doubt of that. She and the boys are all he has of value, and her strong sense of family loyalty is like a magnet to him. And yet he says nothing about her nocturnal meanderings.

In the morning, they meet at the coffeehouse. Nick has lost the key to his rented car and is not certain to make his plane on time. He needs to be in Moscow tomorrow, and is in a state. Marianne says she'll drive him to the airport, if necessary, and he calms down.

A few jokes are made concerning fuzziness about the details of last night's debauchery. Translated into everyday language, this means: "If anything was over the top—you know, emotionally or whatever—just pretend it didn't happen."

They finish their coffees and make their good-byes. Nick is off to see if a spare key can be delivered in time. Marianne is giving a client a massage. William is taking his daughter to a soccer tournament in a neighboring town.

151

That afternoon, Nick has successfully caught his flight out, Marianne has finished her massage, and William is back in town with his daughter and one of her friends—they've been promised a motorboat ride on Lake Casitas, a huge reservoir five miles from Ojai. William calls Marianne to ask if she'd like to come. She says she would.

No onlooker would ever suspect they were anything other than a good-looking, happy family. Marianne is blonde and attractive; the two girls, also beautiful blondes, could be sisters; William is helping the three of them into the boat like a dutiful and attentive husband and father. And yet Marianne has a husband who is jetting away eastward; Elizabeth, the daughter, has a mother who is currently organizing a fundraiser for the Ojai Music Festival; her friend has a father in Ojai and a mother in Santa Barbara; William has a girlfriend who's busy on a project and who would probably have better things to do even if she weren't.

The small, rented boat sputters across the lake at a few miles an hour, periodically tossed about perilously by the hostile wakes of powerboats racing across the water in an inexplicable hurry. Ducks dive for fish and resurface impossible distances away. A few gulls, taking a break from the coast, glide through the air, following a pleasure boat that might throw scraps overboard. A red-tailed hawk floats on thermals above the quiet, surrounding hills, looking for prey.

William, Marianne and the girls find a deserted inlet and maneuver the boat down it. They cut the motor and tie the boat to the overhanging branch of a tree. The girls get out and play in the mud bank, screaming with fear and delight as they sink to their thighs in ooze.

"I think Nick and I truly are alter egos," William observes. He's sprawled across the boat's blue cushions, his toes dangling in the cool water. "It's as though I have been able to experience a certain kind of life without having to actually live it. In a strange way, through Nick I know exactly what it is like to be a successful advertising executive—not because I know him and see what his life has been like, but because I can experience it through his eyes, as if I'd actually gone through it all with him."

Marianne nods in agreement. "Isn't life strange," she exclaims in a dreamy voice. She lights a cigarette and the match makes a fizzing sound as she tosses it into the water. "There you are, two twin souls living out opposite lives so that you can each have the other's experience, and, in the twenty-five years you've known each other, you've never had a heart-to-heart conversation, unless you count last night's awkward demonstrations of affection, which were initiated by alcohol and forgotten by the morning. And the

153

saddest part of it is that you're probably the only friend he's got. Everybody else is either a subordinate, a superior or a rival."

"In a way I am a rival. It's staggering that after all these years we've not once talked about it. He's never spoken to me about my relationship with you, and I've never, not ever, asked you what he says about it to you. Are we bizarre, or what? So now I am going to ask the question, and I can't believe I've never asked it before: 'What does Nick say about you and me?'"

"He never mentions it."

"Never mentions it! What about when we went to Hawaii together?"

"He says: 'Oh, are you going with William? That's nice. Have a great time.' "

"That's all?"

"Yes."

William laughs. "I guess he doesn't think I'm a threat to him."

"He trusts you to take care of me."

William has a sudden insight: "I think I know what it is—I keep you occupied. For as long as you're interested in me, there won't be the emotional space to run off with somebody else—somebody unknown who might take you away for good. I'm a decoy. I stop you looking where the real danger lies. And because we haven't gotten together as a couple in spite of every opportunity to do so, I must seem like a guardian angel to him. When you spend time with me, it must actually make him feel secure."

"I think it does," Marianne agrees.

"And because you've got this whole Italian Catholic thing going, where you can't bear to truly move on —since that would mean a divorce and an official breakup of the family—you have this sort of relationship with me. I respond to certain needs you have; I give you a particular kind of intimacy. And in your heart of hearts you know that we won't elope together—so I give you gratification without danger."

"And what about you?" Marianne asks.

William doesn't answer the question. Instead, he says, "Why have you and I never gotten together? I mean, we act like the happiest couple on earth with the cutest children—why don't we ever make it real? Don't you find it incredible that this is the first time we've really frankly asked that question?"

"What's the answer?"

"I don't know. I guess it isn't written in the stars. It's like Stevie Nicks and Lindsay Buckingham of Fleetwood Mac. They've had this amazing relationship—lovers, songwriters, the incredible experience of rising to rock stardom together—and they still evidently care for each other, and yet somehow they couldn't make it as a couple. It just wasn't meant to be."

"Yes, sometimes things are just not meant to be," Marianne sighs.

The girls are getting tired and bored and want to climb back into the boat. They are muddy and have to be washed first. Then the happy family sets off across the lake, back to the dock, and home to Ojai, where they all disperse to different households, their moment of unity now like a dream.

The following weekend, I am sitting in Libby Park with William, Marianne and Elizabeth. There is a chocolate birthday cake on the picnic table, a thermos of coffee and a bottle of Ojai orange juice. While Elizabeth plays on the swings, William and Marianne chat with me about their lives.

Later, they both go over to the playground to attend to Elizabeth. I pick up the card Marianne gave William. There are two cavemen sitting in front of a birthday cake with many unlit candles on it. The caption reads: "Before fire." One of the cavemen is saying: "Now what?"

I open the card. Marianne has written: *You have been an incredible person in my life, in so many different ways, even though I've hated you at times. I trust you to care genuinely about my deepest well-being. You are a true spiritual friend, not just to me, but—amazingly—to Nick too. Our interlocking lives have been expressions of true caring. Thank you.*

"Yes," I muse, "we are strange creatures. But we're wonderful too."

The Miracle of Intimacy is that it is a process of self-discovery. If we follow its guidance, it will reconnect us with our innermost nature.

Intimacy means being in touch. It is what we desire above all things. We seek it out in sexual contact, but we soon realize, if we are sensitive, that sex enhances our relationship only if it is an expression of already established intimacy; used as a means of creating contact, it merely exacerbates our feelings of aloneness.

When we are intimate with another person, we see and appreciate their deeper nature. We understand what makes them tick; there is a delicious, comforting experience of familiarity.

However, these sensations are so appealing, they are addictive. Because we don't want to lose them, our fears arise and we revert to old patterns of control and manipulation. These patterns, which are attempts to hold onto intimacy, paradoxically cause us to lose it, for intimacy cannot survive in the presence of alienating behavior.

When we experience intimacy with another, we are actually experiencing intimacy with ourselves, and mistakenly attributing it to the other person. When we pine for another, we are in fact pining for ourselves. Only when we understand this, and realize that self-knowledge is our deepest desire, will we look for intimacy in the right place—within. Only then will we enjoy authentic intimacy with others.

"It is one light which beams out of a thousand stars. It is one soul which animates all men."

Ralph Waldo Emerson

COMMUNION WITH DARKNESS
Unanimity

On the surface, we seem to be separate individuals, often with little in common. I feel this way about Hannah. But as our story unfolds, I realize that what we are experiencing must come from a place of deep connection, from the collective soul. At the heart of things, there is a wondrous unanimity.

I MET HANNAH in 1985 on my first day in Ojai, and we formed an instant, though curiously uneasy, friendship. I felt a connection with her, and yet I was always uncomfortable in her presence, as though I was being called upon to give her something emotionally that would be forever beyond my reach. Moreover, she had a restless, searching quality that reminded me of my own pain. I think I sometimes shunned her because she stirred up dragons in me that I wished would remain asleep.

In her twenties, numbed by a loveless marriage and shattered by the ending of an adulterous infatuation, she attempted suicide.

161

"I sat there in my living room," she tells me, "staring at the carpet, which we had had custom dyed in order to match the brick-red print curtains, wondering whether there was anything other than artful decor to look forward to in my life. I had two innocent, faultless children, but I had been living in such pain for so long I now felt I could no longer put them before me.

"Early one morning, before my husband, Marshall, was awake, I walked zombie-like into the children's room. I put Louisa and Peter together in a crib to protect them from seeing what was about to happen, and then went into the bathroom. I fumbled through Marshall's drawer until I found a sharp razor blade. Without hesitation, I drew the blade swiftly and deeply across my wrist, and the next thing I knew I was lying in a pool of blood screaming. The children began to sob and rattle the bars of the crib. Marshall rushed into the bathroom and tried to apply a tourniquet made from his pajamas. My wrist was horribly wounded and I was hysterical with fear and shame.

"Marshall called 911. Shortly afterward, I heard the sirens of the rescue vehicles; they temporarily drowned the cries of pain and terror coming from within our panic-stricken household. I was stabilized in the local hospital and then taken to the county medical center for surgery. As I lay there, waiting to be anaesthetized, I felt shocked by what I had done."

Years later, after extensive therapy that awakened in her the desire to reconnect with her creative nature, she left her children, her husband and their Midwestern suburban life, and drove a van across country to California, where she hoped to find an environment in which she could discover more deeply than before who she truly was.

Thirty years have passed since then, and yet I can still feel traces of the old darkness in her. It scares me. We're sitting opposite each other in the Ojai Coffee Roasting Company, drinking tea. I am uneasy. It's the same uneasiness I have felt around her for the last thirteen years. This time, however, I do something different—I observe the uneasiness without judgment. As I do so, I sense a question welling up in me, as if coming from the uneasiness. Part of me wants to push the question away, but the moment of truth has arrived and I relax and give the question permission to voice itself. As it starts to frame itself in my mind, a small miracle takes place—Hannah answers the question before I speak it. It seems that we both recognize simultaneously that we've reached the turning point.

"You know what I've always felt I wanted from you?" she says. I stare at her. I was on the verge of asking her exactly that. "Your respect," she states simply.

163

Instantly, I see the entire dynamic between us, and tears come to my eyes. Where there was resistance in me, now there is compassion. I see how she has struggled all her life with such painful feelings of unworthiness that she has at times not wanted to go on living. I see that the dragon she stirs up within me is the one named "lack of self-love," and that my discomfort around her is because of this. I see, although I don't understand all the ramifications of it, that we have some ancient contract in which we have agreed to help each other heal.

"I admire you," Hannah says. "You have the intelligence, the ability to communicate and the social ease which I wish I had myself. Your respect would somehow help me."

Another wave of compassion for her passes through me. We are such very different people, with little in common on the surface, and yet we are intimately bonded in our emotional bodies, sharing the same core hurt. I take her in my arms and our tears fall onto each other's shoulders. A process has been engaged that is beyond rational comprehension. It is the fulfilling of a spiritual pact that can only be glimpsed at by the mind.

"You have all those qualities in spades," I tell her. "You have an incredible creative intelligence; you communicate beautifully, not just in words but in dance and in art; and if you sometimes feel difficulty socially, it comes from your lack of self-love, and it would be cured the instant you accepted yourself."

As I speak, I know that my words are not just for Hannah, but also for me. I feel an extraordinary sensation of letting go, a delicious sense of release. This is the first time I've ever let my guard down and spoken warmly to Hannah from the heart. Although a mere expression of appreciation is seldom transforming, in this instance my words appear to have magically triggered a moment of healing. Hannah speaks to me of a new sense of inner strength, an arising of authentic self-appreciation. And I realize that I am experiencing the same thing.

Three days later she calls me. "I'm leaving town," she announces. "I'm moving to Washington State. I have finished my business here in Ojai."

Some of this business has been to spend substantial parts of the last decade volunteering at a local private school. Despite the loving relationships she developed there, one aspect of her experience was a severe challenge—being an academic institution, the place abounds with people who have the sort of verbal and social ease that Hannah believed she lacked; as a result, a sore place in her psyche was being continuously rubbed. However, it appears that the experience was, as with all experiences, a lesson to help Hannah recognize the extraordinary quality and sufficiency of her true nature.

"For the first time in my life," Hannah informs me, "I know that I am the equal of anybody. We are all equal. I do have gifts, and I no longer need to prove it to myself or to anyone else."

So that was the solution to the problem she had been battling for so long—there isn't a problem, and so in a way there isn't a solution. She is a totally complete being, and always has been, and that's all she needed to see. We are all expressions of one spirit: how can there be such things as inferior and superior?

Now Hannah can move to a new home. I hope she finds, inside herself, where the true home lies, the peace and contentment that I wish for her with all my heart.

The next morning she calls me again. "I spoke to my father," she says. "He was angry with me for moving again and doing my customary thing of running away from difficulty. It reminded me of how relentlessly he has, since childhood, tended to unknowingly undermine my self-respect. But instead of getting angry and upset myself, as I usually do, I saw his own vulnerability and felt only compassion for him.

"I just told him calmly that it hurts me when he doesn't trust me or respect my choices, but that I was confident I was doing the right thing for myself."

That evening I run into her in the street. "I've just spoken to my father again," she announces. "His attitude has changed in a remarkable way. He initiated the phone call—which is something he rarely does—and apologized for his anger. He told me that he loved me and supported my choices. It's the first time he's ever expressed that to me."

I look at her in awe. I don't understand everything that has gone on over the last thirteen years, but I know that Hannah and I have both been catalysts, helping each other during a profound moment of healing. I can feel goose bumps forming on my arms at the thought of her reconciliation with her father, for I know this represents an unfathomably deep form of healing.

Hannah gives me more details of her conversation with her father. As she does so, my fanciful imagination conjures up a picture of ten thousand angels in heaven making celebratory music, while the petals of countless lotus blossoms open an unrestrained display of delight.

167

The Miracle of Unanimity is that it dispels the illusion of separation, which is the root of conflict and suffering. How would we behave toward one another, if we knew that in reality we were not separate, but were different manifestations of a single consciousness? How would we feel? Would Hannah have experienced any of the despair that marred her early adult life?

Unanimity means to be of one spirit. Beneath the confusion of our mental chatter—those ever-flowing thoughts composed of stale leftovers from past moments —there is a collective, universally perceptible truth. But we have become accustomed to our conflicts, both those that are known and those that are unacknowledged, and so they feel normal to us. Stilling our minds feels unfamiliar; it makes us anxious. But if we calm our surface thoughts, insights rise up in us, like bubbles of wisdom detaching from the ocean floor, and the knowledge they contain is common to us all.

In this process there is the experience of compassion. We see, not as an idea, but as an actual experience, that each of us in a given situation is struggling with the same issues—even though it does not at first appear this way, since we create dynamics of expression and repression that conceal the deeper truth of our connection.

As we experience our essential oneness, there is a blissful thawing of our negative patterns; the frozen energy, of which they are composed, begins to melt and flow. In that instant, love and understanding, flavored with relief and gratitude, swell up inside us. Conflict and division are understood, not as realities to be overcome, but as illusions to be seen through. Unanimity—the collective soul— is experienced as a delicious facet of reality.

"Gratitude is the sign of noble souls."

Aesop

THE WISH-FULFILLING TREE
Gratitude

David's life began with his mother giving him up for adoption. Many years later, they reconciled. What if, as David's story suggests, this was meant to be? What if we knew that nothing is random? Wouldn't we then have deep appreciation for everything we experienced in life? Wouldn't we be infinitely grateful?

DAVID IS TALL, slim and in the habit of cycling fifty miles before breakfast, which accounts for the greasy breakfast—heart-attack fodder—he is wolfing down with relish. He tells me of a sixty-year-old cyclist with a broken leg, whose doctors proclaimed that he had the circulatory system of a teenager. Only cross-country skiers are healthier, David informs me—in winter that is.

He was raised by adoptive parents. His biological mother delivered him to an adoption center in London when he was three months old, leaving him with no clue to his origins except a beautifully-crafted bassinet that must have cost her all her savings. The bassinet was a message, understood instinctively by David, that she had loved him and was heartbroken to let him go.

I find it difficult to imagine the experience of being raised by adoptive parents. I don't believe that the biological parents are simply egg and sperm donors, and otherwise dispensable. It seems cruel for a mother to carry her baby in her body, feed him at her breast for three months, and then give him away to total strangers. I feel angry with a society in which such a measure should be necessary, and with a woman who would be so disconnected from her natural instincts.

However, who am I to judge? Perhaps, when we are in Heaven making contracts with each other for the next lifetime, we understand the supreme value of self-discovery and willingly agree to whatever worldly experiences are required to achieve it.

In David's life this principle has surely been operating, for his adoption seems to have fueled his spiritual quest. As a young teenager, while most of his peers were obsessing over girls, clothes and rock and roll, he would be hitchhiking to Brockwood Park, in Hampshire, in order to camp out in the rain and hear Krishnamurti talk. When he was seventeen he heard the teachings of Bhagwan Shree Rajneesh for the first time, and then at the age of nineteen he made the long trek to India, in order to meet the master.

"It was 1973, years before any controversy arose about him," David tells me. "He was living in an apartment in Bombay, and as I approached the building, I was feeling a little skeptical; I had been greatly influenced by Krishnamurti, who used to make disparaging comments about gurus, and I had severe doubts about what I was doing. However, I had come all this way to see him, and so I climbed the steps to his apartment and walked into his room. It was completely bare except for a nondescript armchair in which he was sitting. The first instant I set eyes on him, I knew that Rajneesh was no ordinary man—I wasn't going to meet him anywhere else in India, or anywhere else in the world. He looked at you and you knew he could read you like a book. Wherever his gaze turned, he could see the truth of that moment.

"When it was my turn to be introduced, I approached him, and he leaned forward and touched my forehead. At that moment I felt this incredible bliss and my body moved spontaneously. Even now, as I remember it, I can feel tears coming to my eyes. My heart and all my chakras exploded at the same time and my body was arching in bliss. I felt like a totally clear channel for love. There was no thinking; no words could describe it. All I could do was give it out again to the rest of the group. For the next three or four days I felt completely different. If there is such a thing as enlightenment, I felt completely

173

enlightened, although there was no 'I' to feel that. There was just this consciousness. My body felt like it was floating three feet above the ground and everything I did felt like a dance. While this was going on he slipped a mala over my head—the one-hundred-and-eight beads that are a traditional sign of taking sannyas.

"Later, I went up to Rajasthan to attend a meditation camp at Mount Abbu, a hill station, with a cooler climate, which is a paradise of birds, snakes, flowers, trees and waterfalls. He used to hold four meditation camps a year and thousands of people, mainly Indians, would attend, coming from all over the country dressed in white and orange. Two camps were in Hindi and two in English. Mine was in Hindi, but it didn't matter because during the talks I was being touched by a vibration that is beyond words.

"Shortly afterward, Rajneesh's ashram in Poona was founded, and I lived there on and off for a period of nine years. I learned a lot there. Even my mother, who was aghast at my leaving for India at the age of nineteen to hang out with a guru, mellowed in the end—she could see it was benefiting me.

"The ashram was demanding, in a positive way. For example, I used to set off at five in the morning for Bombay in an old diesel van that belched black smoke and drop off other sannyasis at bookstores. Then I'd go to various printing presses and hurry back to meet the sannyasis at lunch and load their purchases into the van. In the afternoon, I'd often have to weave my way through appalling Bombay traffic to the southern tip of the city to visit a cloth shop. At the end of the day, the van was so laden that passengers would have to lie on top of the books and other purchases. I'd drive back to Poona through monsoon rains and arrive there at 1:00 A.M. We'd get a few hours sleep and then be up at dawn to do some other task. We were stretched, and I discovered that it could be a lot of fun—there could be a lot of energy. I learned to say 'Yes' to life. 'Yes, I can do that.' It was very liberating.

"Another job I was given, for about a year, was to stay in his garden all night to guard his room. There had been a few crazy Indians climbing over the fence, which was no mean feat, and some of them got into the house, just like stalkers in Hollywood. The job was given as a meditation. It was called a friction technique—in this case, the friction was between the intense desire to sleep and the conscious commitment to stay alert. Amazing things happen because you're fighting your biology. He would give thousands of different techniques to different people; that was just one.

"One day, I accidentally left in the garden a precious hat he had given me, so I went back in to get it. I came across him having breakfast on his balcony with Vivek, his girlfriend. The garden's like a jungle, with very dense vegetation, and so he didn't see me. My impression was of a very shy, rare deer in the forest which, if it got your scent, or if a twig cracked under your foot, would be gone in a flash. That image of him has always struck me as being the real Rajneesh. When he came out to speak to thousands of people, he put a shield around himself; but on his own, he was incredibly sensitive and retiring.

"I tend to be very suspicious of the reports that came out about him in the States, where he moved after the ashram in India became too small. Scandalous reports were written about him in Poona too—concerning promiscuous sex and so on—and I can assure you they were untruthful. When he wasn't appearing in public, he led what to all of us would be a very austere life. He had one girlfriend, as far as I knew, and that was it. I was in the ashram from 1973 to 1982 and I was amazed by what had been written. It was as though the reporters had never set foot in the place.

"In Oregon, people were critical when he appeared in one of his Rolls Royces. It was an extraordinary sight: thousands of devotees, who were working extremely hard at building a city, would line the roadside; as he drove down the road, a plane overhead scattered rose petals on the pavement in front of him. It was like a Hollywood epic—petals floating down like red snow-flakes against a backdrop of dry mountains and a steel-blue sky.

"People tend to get fixated on lavish displays of materialism on the part of a guru. They see sixty Rolls Royces and project their own issues of self-aggrandizement onto them. They're not seeing the guru at all; they're just seeing reflections of themselves. When I was with him in India, people would question things like his $55,000 diamond watch, and he would usually reply that it was a way of getting at our expectations; it was a method to wake us up. One can be cynical, but I believe what he said was true. You can tell when somebody's into self-glorification, and he wasn't.

"All I can say is that Rajneesh undoubtedly transformed my life, and for that I am eternally grateful. Everything else, to me, is just detail."

After David returned to England from Poona, he met Melissa, the woman who would become his wife. Destiny as I interpret events, engineered their marriage.

It had already made one attempt, in Poona— Melissa had stayed there for six weeks at the same time as David. However, they had inexplicably failed to meet and the first opportunity was lost.

Destiny then tried again, this time choosing a venue so tiny in its proportions—a satellite commune in Brighton, a coastal city in the south of England—that an encounter would be inevitable. Even then, David nearly missed the appointment. Down for the day from London, he completed his business and returned to the train station, having decided to drop the visit to the commune because of the torrential rain that had been pounding the city all afternoon. However, at the station he was suddenly overcome with the urge to turn back—"It was like a hand from the sky telling me to go to the commune," David tells me.

He rang the doorbell and was greeted by an old sannyasin friend from India who gave him some towels to dry off with. The next thing he saw, after his friend and the towels, was a petite, blonde woman who seemed to him so attractive that he assumed she must be married, or have a boyfriend, and have ten other men waiting in line for her.

"When I walked in," David says, "Melissa felt this strange shyness around me. We talked for a while and then the weather cleared up and we went down to the beach for a stroll. I discovered that she was miraculously not accounted for; and it also became clear that she felt the same way about me as I did about her."

They have now been married fifteen years. During the marriage, they have had two children together, and they have lived in England, Canada and now Ojai. Melissa is serving her last year as director of the Oak Grove High School; in her spare time she wages legal battles with David—they are in the process of getting divorced.

It makes me sad that a marriage orchestrated by heaven should be crashing onto the rocks fifteen years later. Is it really for our highest good that so few of our endings appear to be happy ones?

Still, the universe did, in the end, introduce an unmistakable note of compassion into David's life. In his thirties, when he was living in Canada, he had a strong urge to locate his mother; suddenly it seemed inexplicably important to discover his roots. He went through the process they've established in England for adopted children seeking their biological parents and was finally given his birth certificate. He saw that his name at birth had been Colin. The certificate also showed his mother's maiden name and her address.

He wrote to the address and six weeks later got a very friendly postcard back from a Baptist manse (a Scottish vicarage) in Elgin, Scotland. It said: "After much detective work. I have discovered that your mother emigrated to Australia and still lives there under the following name at the following address."

"So, all of a sudden," David tells me, "I had bridged thirty-five years. Melissa and I sat on our bed, staring at the letter, overawed by the enormity of what we were about to do. Melissa found my mother's telephone number from international directory assistance and dialed it. My mother answered the phone and Melissa presented herself as a friend of mine. She told my mother I was looking for her, but gave her every possible avenue of escape, in case it was awkward for her. But my mother was immediately overjoyed at the news and told Melissa she would love to speak to me. So Melissa handed me the phone and I had my first conversation with my biological mother. I was so dazed, I don't remember very much; but I recall that it was like talking to an old friend.

"She wrote me several letters and a few months later came to Canada and stayed with me for three weeks. When I first met her, I remember there being a great deal of familiarity. I found her very easy to be with. We had a lot in common. She had started yoga and she loved long walks in nature. She and her husband owned a small retail store in Australia and on her days off she would walk out into the bush. There were very many things she did that I like to do as well.

180

"We talked a lot. She told me about our Scottish ancestors. She confirmed that she had loved me and that the bassinet had been a sign of her affection. She had breast-fed me for three months and it had been agony for her to let me go. She had considered keeping me, but she was only twenty and Wallace, my father, wasn't the settling down type. He was in the Fleet Air Arm, just like my adoptive father."

The reunion with his mother was an experience David will always treasure. During the three weeks they spent together, their contract with each other in this lifetime was fulfilled. As he drove her back to the airport for her return journey to Australia, there was a sense of completion.

David never saw his mother again. From some deep place of knowledge and compassion, he had been prompted to reconnect with her just in time—for, shortly after her return home, she died, at the early age of fifty-nine. He told me how grateful he had felt that Life had given him this opportunity to reconcile with her.

Today he is faced with a collapsing marriage and challenging finances; but he has been fortified by the early separation from his mother and by all the life experiences that have flowed from it, and he will survive. I begin to sense something quite awesome about his mother's desertion of him; beyond her sad, confused surface nature, I believe her soul was in charge; I believe it was working through her personality to engineer an act of extraordinary self-sacrifice motivated by a divine and loving intent.

David has set up a bookstore on the Internet and sales are showing promise. The business is called "Kalptaru," the name given to heaven's wish-fulfilling tree in Indian mythology. I find the name apt. I believe our dreams are meant to come true, and that apparent obstacles along the way are, as Leslie Merical would say, only signposts guiding us on our path. I believe David, like the rest of us, is being led to Kalptaru, to the ultimate fulfillment of his deepest wishes.

The Miracle of Gratitude is that it reveals the divine hand that orchestrates Life. This is what can be sensed in David's life, which makes his story heart-warming.

What would our experience be if all things really do work together for good? And if death is an illusion? And if there really is an underlying universal intelligence that is all-knowing, all-powerful, omnipresent and infinitely compassionate?

What if waves of divine love lap at the heart of every being at every moment, enticing each one of us individually toward ultimate healing and wholeness? What if we are not who we think we are and have none of the troubles we think we have?

What if every drop of rain, every tear, every loss, every heartache, every disappointment, every failure, every betrayal, every disease—and all things beautiful and uplifting too—what if everything contained an urgent message? What if the world that we apprehend through our five senses were indeed a sort of dream, and like a dream was totally meaningful in every detail?

What if there is a joy-filled perfection at the heart of things that is as yet unseen, but that can be known? What if there is an awareness, lost but recoverable, in which we see the true value of our experiences? What if the truth is that we are destined to sink further and further into our real nature and discover that it is wondrous beyond words?

How would we feel? Wouldn't we be grateful? Inexpressibly grateful?

"Pleasure is the reflex of unimpeded energy."

William Hamilton

THE WAY HOME
Grace

Shirley teaches us that when we are touched by grace, all the blockages in our psyche are dissolved, and our lives begin to flow effortlessly and joyfully. This is the miracle of Grace.

WE ARE SITTING in the walled garden at Greg Penny's house. He and his family are away in St Tropez for six weeks and I am housesitting their palatial property. Greg is a record producer, best known for his award-winning Elton John albums. Orange trees surround the garden. Inside the ivy-lined walls there are roses, willow trees, arbors covered with vines, and three dogs—large, medium and small. The small one is Snowy's twin, lifted straight from a *Tintin* comic; her name is Muñeca, the Spanish word for doll.

Shirley and I are on easy chairs by a large swimming pool, in the shade, sipping well-chilled Chardonnay. Shirley is Petula Clark's twin. Although Petula Clark is a famous singer in Europe, she is relatively unknown in the States and so the resemblance is of little consequence here; strolling down Parisian boulevards, on the other hand (which Shirley and I have done on several occasions), she creates a sensation.

Not that she doesn't create a sensation here as well. Her age is a closely guarded secret—not from vanity, she is quick to assure you; it's to avoid having an image projected onto her—but she looks twenty years younger than she is. She has a mass of curly, very blonde hair and beautiful, somewhat aquiline features. She has a natural air of the patrician about her, initiated by a childhood spent as the daughter of a baseball star and completed by her own stardom as an American figure-skating champion.

By the middle of her life, she had done everything but experienced little fulfillment. However, for whatever mysterious reasons, somewhere inside her the flame of inquiry was flickering, urging her to embark on a psychological and spiritual quest. Never one to do things in half measures, she hung out naked in the hot pools at Esalen (among other places and clothing options) with Alan Watts, Jack Rosenberg, Fritz Perls, Ram Dass and other luminaries of the 1960s counterculture. She quit her affluent life—flying her own planes, hobnobbing with sports stars such as Arnold Palmer, perfectly at home in high society—and became a hardworking professional psychotherapist.

A turning point in her spiritual quest came when she met Vernon Howard. She was browsing in the Bodhi Tree, the Los Angeles metaphysical bookstore, and picked up Vernon's book, *Pathways to Perfect Living.* His words struck an entirely new chord in her. She made inquiries and found that this still relatively un-known spiritual teacher lived and taught in Boulder City, Nevada. Boulder City, Nevada? What was he doing out in the middle of the desert a mere twenty-five miles from that unparalleled shrine to materialism, Las Vegas? How could he be for real?

Nevertheless, in spite of the doubts, she drove across the Mojave Desert in her funny little VW convertible and walked into the sparsely furnished room in which he was giving a talk to twenty people. "After the talk," Shirley tells me, "I went up to him and thanked him. Not just for the talk, but for being here for us all. He looked at me and smiled. That was all. That smile was the warmest … well, I can't put it into words. It was like God smiling at you.

"I looked at him and instantly knew he was absolutely genuine. I knew he was a human being I could totally trust, without even understanding why. It was an unspeakable kind of trust, but it was beyond all doubt.

189

There was a hugeness about him that had nothing to do with who he was as a man.

"We can always find something to criticize about a guru—they buy expensive cars or they are in a relation-ship we disapprove of—and Vernon was no exception to this. He was very austere in his personal habits, which I liked, but his look and his emphatic way of speaking didn't fit my fantasy of what my spiritual teacher would he like. Krishnamurti, a handsome Indian with noble features, looked much more the part.

"To appreciate a teacher, a suspension of judgment is required. Not a removal of judgment; that's something different, found in cults. A suspension of judgment is a willingness to set aside immediate impressions in order to allow the deeper truth of a situation to reveal itself.

"A suspension of judgment is, in fact, an indispens-able technique for all aspects of our lives. It means we stop assuming we know what's best for us. Every one of us is in pain and wants to end it. We try to do so by seeking money, a mate or even spirituality; or by escaping into distractions, dreams, drugs and denial. We don't question our strategy until we hit bottom and begin to suspect that everything we've been doing has been in vain, and that we have no ace left up our sleeve. In that moment when we give up, something comes in and replaces our hope and our efforts. We don't know where it came from and we don't question it; we just know it. It's Grace.

"Grace is in the moment. It is part of the ever-flowing current of life. Our conditioning, which is the past moving toward the future, can't touch this place whose location is the present, and the more we spin around looking for it the less we're going to find it. Thus, Grace comes to us of its own volition, not ours. Our limited nature rebels at this loss of personal control, but when we experience it, there is nothing we want more. It is the end of all our seeking. Our frozen energy melts and our lives become full of ease and beauty.

"Grace brings certainty. Before, our certainty was not authentic. We believed in our answers, but when nothing turned out as we expected, we moved into uncertainty. That's when we started to look for deeper meanings. True certainty is deep understanding, complete understanding. It arises from contact with Grace, whose intrinsic nature is certainty.

"In a state of Grace, life with all its pains and struggles turns into joy—'joy,' not 'happiness,' because joy is not the result of an exterior effect. Unlike happiness, it does not come and go; it doesn't depend on the external situation; it is present in a luxury estate in Ojai under a clear sky and in a slum in Calcutta in the monsoon. Being independent of these phenomena, it can be trusted.

191

"The experience of Grace happens automatically. We can't force it. We can't read about Grace and say, 'OK, I'm going to start doing that now.' We can't run after Grace—it dwells in a place that is inaccessible to our everyday minds—but we can see things as they are. We can see what is false as being false. If we do this, Grace will appear. That's a promise, a prayer that is always answered.

"Grace is supreme value. If we don't value above all else the spirit that animates everything 'out there,' then we're not seeing things as they really are and we're going to suffer. There's nothing wrong with having and appreciating spouses, children, friends, family and even money; but whatever we're attached to 'out there' is sooner or later going to let us down. People are going to leave, die or argue with us; places and finances are going to change. Only when Grace enters our lives will we be able to truly love and appreciate everything we have. For as long as we mistakenly believe that our well-being depends on transient things, we will suffer."

Shirley pauses. A look of pain comes into her eyes. The conversation has resuscitated a sorrowful memory: Bert, her adored cat, died recently, and she is still grieving. Shirley is a woman who's spent most of the last twenty years steeped in spiritual inquiry, and yet she freely admits that she cried for a week over his death.

"Bert was filling my holes," she says. "I wasn't aware of it, but he filled my loneliness. It was like losing one's baby. I knew enough not to dismiss it as some silly incident. The tears that came were not just for Bert, though; they opened a place in my heart and deepened my realization that God's the only one—only He will do. If I lean on anything else, I become disconnected from the true source of security, well-being and fulfillment. It's as simple as that.

"Life will always bring us these experiences; it will constantly reveal to us the pain of our attachments and mistaken beliefs. It does so not to cause us suffering, but to show us the way home."

The Miracle of Grace is that it puts an end to our personal effort. Action is taken, but it is not motivated by our individual will.

Shirley's description of Grace corresponds closely to something I experienced one afternoon while I was sitting by a creek with a friend. I felt an effervescent, dancing flow of energy within me. It stayed for several hours, and it ran the show in every way. It filled my conversation, inspiring me with the perfect words to say. When it was time to be silent and experience the beautiful natural surroundings, Grace guided me in that too. If I needed insights about my life, it caused them to arise effortlessly in my mind. It was there in every instant, for every event, whether important or mundane.

Throughout, there was an unforgettable experience of love and total serenity—but passion and energy too—of omniscient intelligence and unlimited creativity. There was no compulsion to receive this energy into my being. It was totally in my power to block it out or move away from it, and indeed in the end, as I slipped out of the state of hyper-openness, that's what happened. But while this life energy coursed through me, I knew there was nothing I could want more. It was a state of inconceivable delight.

"*Life is a game played on us while we are playing other games.*"

Evan Esa

BLESSINGS IN THE VEGETABLE GARDEN
Life

Patrick is depressed, unemployed, and creatively frustrated. But a small miracle takes place in a vegetable garden, and he gains a new perspective on Life.

THE OAK GROVE SCHOOL vegetable garden is overrun with weeds and Patrick has volunteered an hour a day to help clear it.

The school was founded by the Krishnamurti Foundation of America, and began life as an experiment in enlightened education. Krishnamurti lived part of each year in Ojai during a sixty-five-year period and he gave talks each spring in the delightful grove of oak trees from which the school took its name. At that time of year the grass would still be green and the trees would glisten with a coating of mist that evaporated in the heat of the late morning sun. A blue heron would strut around its nest importantly and there would be a stillness in the air that could almost be tasted.

Krishnamurti sat straight, but relaxed, on a wooden chair, and his words seemed to materialize from a vast reservoir and float through the air with perfect precision. And yet it wasn't what he said that moved you most; it was a presence that he brought to the gathering, an energy that filled the grove and lightened your soul. Mary Zimbalist, his long-time personal assistant, once said that he changed the energy everywhere he went, and that people who didn't even know he had stayed in a particular lodging would comment on the uplifting atmosphere.

Patrick met Krishnamurti in the early 1980s, when Patrick first moved to the valley. He and his wife were invited to lunch. The great man stood humbly to one side, while the six guests served themselves from the buffet and took their places. Then he put a small quantity of salad on his own plate and joined them. During the meal the conversation turned to the subject of Christian fundamentalists. Everybody criticized them in mocking tones, contemptuous of their fanaticism and hypocrisy. Even Krishnamurti joined in.

Patrick listened to the repartee with a growing feeling of disgust. Who were these people to condemn others who, like themselves, were making a sincere, if misguided, effort to lead good lives and know God?

And what did this say about the revered teacher, that he would stoop to ridicule?

Finally, Patrick could contain himself no longer. "Christian fundamentalists are, for the most part, doing the best they can," he exclaimed. "Can't we acknowledge their intent? They're just trying to lead decent lives; and if, in the process, they make mistakes or are deluded in any way—so what? If you were walking down a dark alley at midnight and a dozen young men were coming toward you, wouldn't you he relieved to discover that they were returning from a fundamentalist meeting? Let's give credit where credit is due."

Krishnamurti looked softly at Patrick and said nothing. The others coughed, ate, scratched their heads and exhibited other forms of avoidance. Nobody wanted a serious discussion.

By the end of the meal, Patrick had iconoclastic feelings firmly entrenched in his heart: he'd moved to the valley in order to be in the presence of the master, and it seemed that all he'd found was a petty-minded old man. When it was time to say good-bye, however, something special happened that Patrick would never forget. Krishnamurti enfolded both Patrick's hands in his and looked him in the eyes. In that instant Patrick was transported into another world.

"It was," he says, "as though I were floating through this ocean of incredibly sweet, loving stillness—an indescribable gentleness. I knew then that anything I might see him do, or hear him say, was just on the surface. This man was connected to something infinitely deeper than visible behavior.

"He expressed the wish that my new life in the valley would be prosperous, and made a few other pleasantries that I've forgotten. Then he let go of my hands, and I thanked him. He held my wife's hands in the same way, and she reported to me afterward that she had experienced exactly the same phenomenon as I had. He had given us something very special— a sort of blessing."

Patrick's life hasn't prospered yet, despite the blessing. An insane infatuation with another woman recently cost him his marriage and his children. Although he has a Ph.D. in English and a wonderful way with language, he has not yet realized his dream, which is to make money with his pen. Recently he quit a "temporary" job as a mail carrier. He started it fifteen years ago, just to pay the rent for a while, but the next thing he knew the job had expanded into a career. It was when he found himself calculating how many years were left until early retirement that he realized how desperately off track he had gotten.

Now he is unemployed, but determined to finally make his living in a way that expresses his talent and his passion. He is confident that one day his poetry and other writings will bear fruit. In the meantime he wants to start up a "Vanity Autobiography Service." For one very reasonable fee he will ghostwrite your autobiography and print three thousand copies, thus providing you with an inexhaustible supply of unwelcome Christmas gifts. He hasn't found a client yet, but he's sure there must be hundreds of takers out there.

Still, he's worried and depressed. Although the business idea raises his spirits, he is acutely aware of his rapidly dwindling finances and of the statistical improbability of making his living as a writer.

Patrick has volunteered at the school in order to get a change of scenery from his shabby, dark apartment, where he would otherwise spend most of the day. Standing by a weed-covered bed of Swiss chard, ready to begin weeding, he senses Krishnamurti's presence filling him; as he bends down and pulls out a thistle standing two-feet tall, strange metaphysical thoughts drift into his mesmerized mind:

Soil represents the mind, and the weeds that grow in it are like false ideas. The vegetables are truths. I notice that weeds are pulled out more easily when

they are young. Once there are too many weeds, you can no longer see the vegetables.

Sometimes I pull out vegetables, thinking they're weeds. And vice versa—sometimes I overlook weeds, thinking they're vegetables. It's easy to be confused.

Weeds are uprooted more easily if the soil is airy and moist, just as false ideas are more readily detected in a mood of warm light-heartedness.

Weeds must be extracted by the root, otherwise the roots remain in the soil and the weeds grow back. Also, some weeds are thorny, but when grabbed by the root, they don't prick you.

A clean bed with rows of green vegetable stems and nothing else is beautiful in a Zen-type way. A weedy bed is cluttered. On the other hand, I can also look at the whole vegetable garden, weeds and all, and find it perfectly right and beautiful. It's important to bear in mind that everything's a question of perspective.

During the weeks that follow, Patrick pulls out thirty barrow-loads of weeds from beds of onions, beets, carrots, peas, lettuce, broccoli, cabbage, cauliflower and potatoes. After three weeks, he notices a definite improvement in his state of mind; he is feeling lighter and more buoyant and much more optimistic. It seems that a lot of his own negativity has been uprooted along with those weeds.

"So this work," Patrick tells me, "although unpaid, has given me its own precious gift. I did not come to it with any expectation of a reward—on the contrary, it just seemed like a way to get sweaty and muddy—and yet it contained something very valuable for me. It put me back in touch with the beauty that's intrinsic to any given moment. I just needed to change my perception, as in that famous optical illusion in which the drawing of an old lady magically changes into a picture of a gorgeous young woman. There I was, so darned sure that my reality was that of an unemployed mail carrier with a Ph.D., with nothing but regret for the past, depression in the present, and anxiety about the future. But my time in the vegetable garden somehow snapped the fixation, the hypnosis. Suddenly, I turned into this indefinably marvelous creature, playing with the life-filled soil and plants that make up this miraculous planet, this strange home of ours floating in an immeasurable universe amongst countless stars.

"I think this was part of the lesson I learned from Krishnamurti all those years ago at lunch: Life is playing

203

a loving game with us; it coaxes us into getting fixated on an illusion, and then it suddenly pops up elsewhere and says, 'Look, this is the way things really are!'

"Life plays games that are deep and mysterious. And one of its preferred games is quite delightful. It loves to deliver blessings to us in the most unlikely places, at the most improbable times."

The Miracle of Life is that it is a game. This is not an invitation to be flippant or to engage in wrongdoing. Life can still be taken seriously, but it is liberating to know that everything we experience is intentional and designed for our benefit.

Life loans us a body. It is the only thing we can be sure to keep for a lifetime. We are born into this world equipped with a small number of built-in rules, called principles. They are self-evident and clear, if we listen to our conscience.

The object of Life's game is that we remember who we are. People and experiences are mirrors to help us achieve this.

There is no right or wrong, only understanding or ignorance. There is no punishment, only feedback.

We have forgotten all this, but we can remember any time we choose.

"Order is heaven's first law."

Proverb

ENTER THE SPA GODDESS
Order

A brief encounter with Marielle brings up in me the sorrow of all the partings I have ever experienced in my life. But the truth is there's order in the universe. Order is a miracle which, when seen clearly, banishes sorrow.

MARIELLE is in perpetual motion, hopping across the world from one five-star resort to another, following her passion of introducing ancient healing techniques to top-notch spas. Between assignments as a spa consultant, she is still on the go, studying with exotic teachers on every continent. Presently, she is en route from San Francisco to Albuquerque to spend a few weeks with one of the world's foremost Vedic astrologers; as her journey takes her within fifteen miles of Ojai, she makes a detour to visit an English architect she met at a café in Bali.

I run into her at the coffeehouse and there is an instant connection. She is a curious mixture of the efficient and the esoteric; dressed in Balinese clothes that

207

drip otherworldly shades of blue and purple, she types e-mail messages into her laptop with the business-like air of a senior vice-president. She tells me she's the "Spa Goddess." If you're ready for her, she says, she'll descend on your establishment and take it into a new dimension of healing. It's no longer enough to luxuriate in mineral baths and ease tense shoulders on the massage table. Spa-goers are seeking more than a "lube-'n'-go" massage; they want sessions that change their reality. And so Marielle helps spas introduce an array of time-honored techniques, such as Ayurvedic treatments or Balinese massage, that will ultimately transform these places into the wellness centers of the twenty-first century.

I tell her that I understand perfectly what she's doing. We are at the dawn of a new era in planetary consciousness; the celestial finger is beckoning to us all, even to senior vice-presidents and their spouses taking a break from corporate America. We are all being invited to attend to our spiritual health, and this means getting serious. No longer is it enough simply to relax sore muscles. We need to realize that our bodies are biological suits of armor, storehouses for our traumas and their associated defense mechanisms. We're clanking around in our lives, one great bundle of metallic protection, separated from ourselves and each other without knowing it. Our qualities are unreal, a facade; they're phony constructions that we hide behind. Our strength conceals our vulnerability, our assertiveness conceals our confusion, our material abundance conceals our inner emptiness, and our love conceals our fear. The road to health requires taking off the suit of armor and facing the wounds it protects. When we do this, a miracle occurs: the wounds are healed and our true nature—which is one hundred per cent real, alive and good, and which contains our qualities in their authentic form—is uncovered.

So this is what we can all aspire to. This is what will transform our lives and our planet. And this is the process to which all places of healing, including fancy spas, should pay attention.

Manage a spa and don't know where to start? Then call in the Spa Goddess. Under her guidance, your resort will become a place of the new millennium. As pleasant as it is to take off our clothes and plunge into hot springs, this will no longer be enough. In tomorrow's world we will seek out beautiful sanctuaries in which we can take off our armor, sink into our being and become whole.

Marielle has pluck and a sense of purpose. She is a dynamo. She tells me she only sleeps a few hours a night. I wonder whether she is just another neurotic do-gooder, but I sense that she has been through many a dark night, released much of her "stuff," and is now simply expressing a natural, untrammeled energy.

We spend an hour together in the coffee shop. The conversation is fast and furious, and ideas zing across the table at ever-increasing speeds. I think I am inter-viewing Marielle, but I realize she is interviewing me. She asks about my dreams and aspirations, and we talk about my two children in Switzerland who have been separated from my daily life for over a decade. I feel sadness as we touch on this topic, and quickly change the subject.

I ask for her business card and she presents me with a miniature work of art—her photo screened in the background in teal, under a purple logo of her company name, "Healing Choices." Using a robin's egg blue ink pen, she makes a list on the back of the card of books she thinks will interest me. The titles do intrigue me and they create a sense of recognition between us, a feeling that we are from the same tribe; I mention this to her and she is delighted. She takes a bulging day-planner out of a tote bag and withdraws a crisply folded article she wrote in Bali and has been sending to friends. The title is *21st-Century Pilgrims: Who is my tribe?* The following extracts catch my eye:

Unlike the traditional community, defined by geographical boundaries shaped by history and handed down through the generations, my community is made up of people sharing an inner geography of common beliefs and values. I run into these sisters and brothers on my pilgrimages around the planet—Vedic students in Sydney; budding artists in Bali; foreign language teachers in Japan; writers in Bangkok, following in the footsteps of Somerset Maugham and Joseph Conrad.

We find mirrors in each other, definitions of who we are that give structure to the inner geography and a way to recognize fellow members of the tribe, Silently holding up our badges of membership, our markers are discovered in conversation rather than by a uniform or coordinates on a map: we are seriously concerned with psychology, spiritual life, self-actualization, self-expression; we share a love for the foreign and exotic; we enjoy mastering new ideas; socially concerned, we are strong advocates of ecological sustainability Our clan's members tend to be "leading edge" thinkers and creators. We perceive all too clearly the systemic problems of today, all the way from the local level to the national and to the planetary.

211

To the consternation of our families, our less-traveled path leads to a variety of workshops, "bizarre" communities, gatherings, meditation centers, spiritual retreats, hot spring resorts, healers, shamen and a plethora of techniques to reconnect with our bodies, emotions, intuition. Time-tested right-brain rituals —like music, art, dance, bodywork, poetry and story-telling—bring us closer to an inner sense of home than the confines of a church pew ever did.

Looking to find ourselves, we bump into others on the same quest, sometimes in the oddest places. Those we click with frequently become lifelong friends; yet sometimes the spark is there for just the length of the airplane or train ride, and then we're off again on our own paths, both having been nurtured by the connection, but not needing to cling to it.

Whoever we are, this tribe, this clan of seekers, we are not alone, even though we may have felt that way at times. Membership is open to all; there are no exclusions, except self-imposed ones. More and more of us are shedding our routines, our scripts, our houses and our traditional jobs, and are taking to the road, literally or figuratively. We are finding that our path is one and the same. We are the 21st-century pilgrims.

Marielle finishes her mocha, topped with whipped cream and trails of chocolate shavings (chocolate, she says, is the one addiction she allows herself) and announces that it is time for her to go. I accompany her to her station wagon, which is packed to the roof with her belongings. Though our friendship is just one hour old, we hug each other like best friends. We have discovered that we both have birthdays next week, just two days apart, and we wish each other "Happy Birthday."

She gets into her car and starts the engine. Then she leans out of the window and, with a warm smile and a mischievous wink, blows me a kiss. She pulls out slowly into the traffic and drives off for another adventure.

In spite of our instant connection, I know we may never meet again. A faint sadness passes through me. I think of my life, filled with an endless succession of meetings and partings—friends, lovers, wives, relatives, children—and I feel the strange sorrow that permeates all my relationships, and indeed my whole existence. Everything is in such tremendous flux.

I know that unity is at the heart of things, and that separation and impermanence are illusions. However, standing on the dusty Ojai sidewalk at 11:30 A.M. on a Tuesday morning watching Marielle's Toyota dwindle to a point on the long road heading eastward, the idea of "essential unity" does not console me.

I go back into the coffeehouse and engage a stranger in conversation. We talk about the weather. I say to the man: "It never ceases to amaze me that Californians discuss the weather as much as the English do. At least in England the weather is infinitely variable, and therefore new dimensions to the subject can be brought into the conversation forever; but in California three hundred days of every year are indistinguishable from one other; you would have thought that a couple of discussions each winter would cover everything there was to say on the matter."

My interlocutor is looking around the coffeehouse as if wondering whether there is a more interesting conversation going on at another table. I realize I am being excessively English—that is to say, being pompous, supercilious, didactic and fond of interminable discussions about all matters meteorological.

I must be wheeling my English conditioning onto the stage as a defense mechanism; I do that when I'm trying to avoid painful feelings. I take a deep breath and relax; immediately I see the real issue. Marielle's gentle probing into my psyche has touched the wound around my absent children. I glance at the clock: it's now noon; so it is 9:00 P.M. in Switzerland. I realize that, if I hurry, I can call my children there before bedtime. To the bewilderment of the stranger, I rush out of the coffeehouse with barely a word of goodbye. As I drive home, a sense of peace settles over me. This telephone call is what I have needed to do this morning; it has been niggling at the edges of my consciousness and finally it has been acknowledged.

I think of Marielle on her way to Albuquerque. I am grateful for the brief connection; there is no longer any sadness around it. It was perfect just the way it was—a stimulus to reconnect with one of the deepest issues in my life.

I think of my two children in Switzerland, raised for the last twelve years without me, and realize that something is different—my thoughts, for the first time since they and their mother left America, are free of pain. At last, I can think of what happened without resistance or anger. As though I have just shed my armor in one of Marielle's resorts, a soothing sense of trust settles into me; in a deep place—deeper than my conscious understanding—I begin to feel that everything even the separation from my beloved children, is perfect just the way it is.

A celestial alarm has sounded inside the intricate mechanism of my spiritual growth, and a moment of healing has been bestowed on me. Why my life took the course it did, leading to this moment, I have no idea; but suddenly I catch a glimpse of something that is loving and compassionate beyond all my dreams—I see that every instant of my life has been choreographed for my good and for the good of those affected by me; I understand that each and every experience, including a brief—but catalyzing—encounter with the Spa Goddess, has been infused with a higher purpose designed for my ultimate well-being and for that of my loved ones. There is, thank God, order in the cosmos.

As I walk into my house and head for the phone, a wonderful sense of peace, a greater feeling of stillness than I have ever experienced before, descends on me. "It's all OK," I whisper to myself, and I know that I truly mean it.

The Miracle of Order is that it makes us divine, for orderliness is one of the attributes of the Light.

Order is the natural expression of an integrated being. There is comfort and strength in every form of order —practical, moral and interpersonal. Order is knowing our vision and marshalling the necessary resources to achieve it. Order is keeping our word, to ourselves as well as to others. Order is disciplining our habits, efforts and wishes. Order means organizing our life and managing our time. Order means light and peace, inward liberty and free command over ourselves.

However, order is impossible for as long as we are split within ourselves. We cannot have order when warring factions within our psyche insist on moving in opposite directions. Only when we connect with our essence, which is unified, can we enjoy order.

Then all our energy moves in a single direction and we become awesomely effective. We discover that order is power.

"He who does not love does not know God; for God is love."

1 John 4:8

A SYMPHONY OF HEALING
Love

Love is not an abstraction, but a tangible energy that bestows countless blessings on us. In this concluding story, I am the lucky recipient of Love's miraculous healing power.

ALLEE IS TALL, blonde, clear and beautiful. She wears spring dresses with floral patterns. She is unashamedly feminine. Looking at her, I know the truth about femininity. Women are like musical instruments. The Female Principle, that floods our planet from the moon and the stars, plays through them. Women who are clear channels for this music have an exquisite beauty; a beauty that transcends their physical features, their age, their sexuality; an eternal, archetypal beauty.

In this land of misguided equality, I want her to stand on a coffeehouse table and be seen by every female customer. "This is a pure woman. This is the pure

219

expression of femininity. This is a loveliness that comes from heaven."

Instead, I ask her what she wants to talk about. In soft, lilting tones, her voice mellowed by a childhood spent in Virginia and Georgia, she tells me she could talk about anything. And I believe she could.

I suggest we start with what she does for a living.

"I have been given the gift of channeling divine energy into the genetic imprint, into the coding locked in the cellular system. This means I can discover hidden blocks that prevent people from recognizing their true divine essence, and then initiate their release. My intention is to awaken divinity in everybody I touch and work with … how's that for putting it in a nutshell?"

I reply that her statement will make it into the book unedited. She laughs loudly. Local Hero is opening and the sound of her laughter mingles with the *splat!* of a mop with which a teenage girl is cleaning the patio.

"Before a client arrives," she explains, "I spend a great deal of time preparing myself. I've set up my home as a temple to anchor in divine energy and whoever walks into that temple begins to feel the energy. At the beginning we just sit and talk for a while and I get them into the space to receive the work that I do. Then they lie on a massage table and I work with Spiritual Response Therapy. This is a technique brought through by a brilliant man named Robert Detzler. It's a system of divination that allows you to go into the subconscious and the cellular system and look at blocks—beliefs, genetic imprints, identifications and past life memories —that influence behavior which may no longer be for the highest good and is ready to be cleared from that particular being. Once the blocks have been revealed, I use massage and anointing with oils to clear them.

"The technique is quick. It's real quick—miraculous. You can clear multiple issues in one session. But you're not going to clear your entire being. I won't claim that. It's not a 'one-shot-fix-everything-enlightened-master-walk-out-into-the-world-and-there-you-are' event. For as long as we are in a body there will be things to heal.

"It's a challenge being human. We truly are spiritual beings having a physical experience, and as such we are unlimited—the essence of who we are is completely unlimited. When we come in as children we are separate from nothing and no one, and we know that. Then an experience comes along that triggers the illusion that we are separate. It's part of the human experience. We know we're not separate, but the illusion, which is perpetuated by society and family, overpowers us. Until humanity is healed of this, we will all continue to uncover issues originating from that illusion."

Allee confesses that she herself has been dealing with this issue in her relationship, which is in its dying phase. It's been the most challenging relationship she's ever been in, and she's faced every dark emotion imaginable: abandonment, betrayal, insecurity, jealousy. But she views it all as an opportunity to know herself.

"In our interactions with others," she says, "if we have a judgment, if we have a belief, if we have an emotion about an issue or a statement or a behavior, it's because we have that issue going on within ourselves. And so a relationship is a wonderful tool for looking at what our stuff is. If we don't have a charge on a person's negative behavior—if we don't have emotion around it—then it's not ours; it's OK. We can let the being have whatever experience he or she needs to have.

"For me, underneath every issue that arises in my life, there is one fundamental issue: separation from God. This was brought home to me poignantly when my beloved master died, six years ago."

A new intensity and focus enters her voice. I feel a tingle down my spine. I sense that we are getting to the heart of her heart, and I can feel my own heart beat a little faster. I ask her to tell me about her master.

"A very dear friend of mine," Allee says, "told me of a man whom her uncle had encountered in Mexico, who was supposed to be a great teacher and a great master—an avatar. She said he was coming to the United States—to Ojai—and that it was an incredible opportunity for me to meet a master.

"I said: 'OK, I'll check this out.' Then I started hearing all kinds of stories about him and I became very skeptical. I remember driving over to meet him. I was with a girlfriend and we were saying: 'Who does this Mexican think he is?' We were being very, very irreverent. Suddenly, in the middle of all this irreverence, I looked at my friend and I said, 'You know, the weirdest thing is happening to me—my heart is beating so fast I feel like I'm going to meet, a lover.' And she said, 'You know, so is mine!'

"So we get to this friend's house, where the master is—his name was José Luis. The friend says, 'Oh come in, come in. He's just sitting talking right now.' We walk in and here's this very young, very handsome man with long hair, beautifully dressed in impeccable clothes. There were all these people gathered around him and he was just laying in the living room on a beanbag chair. I walked in and thought, 'There's nothing special here —I mean what's the big deal? What's all the hullabaloo about?'

"Then she led me over and brought me within about eight feet of him. She started to introduce me, and as he turned he looked me in the eyes. When his

223

eyes met mine it was as if somebody had sent a thunderbolt down into the top of my head and shot a million volts through it. My body started to shake uncontrollably and I started to cry. I fell to my knees and I sobbed continuously for about three hours. I just knew who he was, and that I had lived my entire life for him. I had never felt so full of love or been loved so completely by anyone. I knew that this was what I'd been looking for.

"I spent the next ten days that he was in Ojai with him. I didn't leave his side. That was the start of our relationship. From then on, I was with him every possible moment. I gave up my home, packed up some suitcases and was on the road. I traveled around the world with him—Mexico, South America, Israel, Egypt and Hawaii. I was his angel. I was the one who, when he was in pain, would come and rub my hands over him and calm him. I'd soothe him at night when he would process. That lasted four years."

I ask if they were lovers and she replies: "We were never intimate as lovers, but it was every kind of relationship. José Luis awakened God consciousness in me. He awakened me to my own mastery. He awakened in me my ability to be loved. He did that by just being there. No techniques. It was a vibration. When you came into his vibration it happened.

"When he first moved into his mastery, he was told that he would only live to be thirty-three. He was told that this would be the length of his mission, his role here, but he didn't know how he would die.

"He was traveling in Amsterdam and he was walking through the red light district and a prostitute came up to him and said, 'I have a gift for you.' He'd never been with a prostitute before. In fact he hadn't had sex in years. When it came time to pay, the prostitute said, 'No, it's my gift. It's a gift.'

"A year later he developed AIDS. It was really an incredible thing, a modern-day crucifixion. Many people around him, including myself, had major judgments about AIDS, but his illness took us completely out of any prejudice about it. We developed a great deal of compassion around the disease; it was a beautiful thing.

"There are always lessons in life, even for a master. He suffered, but he did it with dignity and that was one of the gifts he gave to us—showing us how to die with dignity.

"He also taught us not to judge. One time we were in the barrios in Rio de Janeiro. I remember seeing a little child of three in the gutter, wearing a tattered orange dress, looking for food. I pointed her out sadly to José Luis, and he said, 'Who are you to judge her experience? Who are you to say her soul has not chosen the most perfect experience for her?'

225

"That had a great impact on me. I really had to take a look at how I judge everyone's experience in relation to mine. I suffer too. I have painful experiences. I cry myself to sleep. It's all relative. My suffering is no less than anyone else's suffering and their suffering is no less than mine. We feel pain when we need to feel pain and we feel it to the level we need to feel it. Only to know it. Because it's a part of life.

"José Luis died in Mexico. I left the day before. I knew he was going to die the next day, and I knew it was OK for me to leave. I had completed. I was with him in my dream when he died; it was 4:44 A.M., and at 4:45 I was awake. An hour later I got a phone call from my friend who was at his side when he passed away.

"I was in an altered state then, and felt almost elated; but later I experienced a lot of grief—the pain of separation, of once again being abandoned. He had been magic for me. He had been my best friend in every way, and my love. He had helped me be in contact with myself in more fulfilling and life-enhancing ways than I had ever experienced before. And so when he was gone the loss was cosmic."

A few days after our meeting, I telephone Allee for a professional appointment; I want to experience her healing techniques; I believe her when she claims that she has an exceptional gift.

I drive out to her home with a sense of great expectation. Four months ago, Leslie Merical sat with me at the Ojai Coffee Roasting Company and urged me to write *Everyday Miracles*. She promised that it would bolster my self-trust, and she was right. Once the treatment with Allee is completed, the last piece of the book will be finished; I am already beginning to feel a delicious sense of accomplishment.

My life has undergone many changes in many different ways since I began writing the book. I have been exposed constantly to the helping hand of serendipity, and have begun to trust it; I have received tremendous personal inspiration from everybody I have met; I feel incomparably better about myself and my life than when I first started. Leslie told me that unexpected gifts would manifest from writing the book, and again she was right. I couldn't wish for more than what I have already received. If *Everyday Miracles* serves as an inspiration to others, that will be a delightful bonus.

Allee's cottage is tucked away in the orange groves in the east end of the valley. Crystals of all kinds are arranged on a table—ruby, lavender quartz, topaz and many more—all of different sizes and shapes. She shows me a large spherical crystal that she says was shown to her in a vision when swimming with dolphins. Later, in magical circumstances, the crystal was presented to her. She says, quite matter-of-factly, that it comes from another planet. Before I have time to question the assertion, she hands it to me and invites me to look at the colors inside. I hold the crystal near a lamp and can see nothing but pretty reflections of the white light. "It's lovely," I comment lamely. Then I suddenly find the correct angle and a kaleidoscope of colors comes alive deep within the stone. They seem like a rainbow from a different universe—the reds are vermilion and scarlet, the yellows are golden, the greens are deep and glisten like an Irish landscape. I've never seen anything like it.

On another table there is a collection of essences. There must be one hundred different bottles—frankincense, wild rose, lemon, jasmine. The air is a symphony of exquisite smells. I breathe in deeply and can feel the aromas soothing my body, aided by the soft but evocative music that's playing.

On the walls are pictures of José Luis. I had imagined him to he perfectly handsome—in an off-putting sort of way. But he is offbeat handsome—in an appealing sort of way. I would have liked him if I had known him.

Allee leaves the room so that I may undress and lie on a massage table under a sheet. When I am settled she calls from the next room, asking if she may enter. She stands by the table and picks up a gold cross on a chain. Seven jewels, representing the seven colors of the rainbow and thus the seven chakras, are set into the cross. She holds it over me by a thin gold chain and it begins to swing like a pendulum. Guided by its movements, she starts her diagnosis. For half an hour she talks about my issues of self-worth, lack of appreciation, powerlessness and countless other blockages. She relates them to all different parts of the time scale—childhood, inside the womb, in previous lives—and to every type of body—physical, mental, emotional and spiritual.

As I listen to her, I know she has truly contacted my life issues. Sometimes she speaks of blocks I am not aware of, and I decide it's OK to trust her.

Then the therapy begins. She tells me that there is nothing for me to do except surrender. My only task is to let go. It sounds reassuringly simple.

She places a small beanbag over my eyes and then starts to massage my feet. Time during the next several hours becomes suspended as she launches into a virtuoso, orchestral performance on me. Massaging me, caressing me, holding me, rocking me, anointing me with oils, rubbing fragrances under my nose for me to inhale, sounding Tibetan bells whose etheric, tinkling vibrations ripple through my emotional body, invoking (silently) angels and guides and—above all—transmitting through her hands waves and waves of absolutely tangible love.

I go into an altered state in which I am awake but have vivid dream images floating in and out of my mind. People and scenes flash by. Weird symbolic pictures arise, as when I see her take a phial of liquid from my left foot and throw the contents away.

Then she reaches my stomach, at the level of the third chakra. Ominous rumbling sounds begin. I can feel this hard lump like a cannonball, but it is not in my physical body—it's in my emotional body. Allee is barely touching my flesh, and yet it feels as if she is kneading this cannonball with all the strength she can muster. I realize that I am being called upon to surrender, as per instructions. I see now that this might be more difficult than I had imagined. In fact, it seems impossible that any degree of letting go will ever allow this dense knot of frozen energy to thaw.

I begin to pray. I pray to God to have mercy on me and help me heal. I pray to the angels and guides that I feel all around me to show me how to surrender. The prayers come from such a deep place I can almost believe they originate in the emotional block itself. "Please, help me. I know this block has been a terrible source of suffering all my life. I know it has caused me incredible pain and led me to cause others pain. Please release me from this."

These prayers and thoughts run instantly through my mind, and within a fraction of a second there is a response. I feel the presence of the angels around me intensifying—I can hardly believe it is true, but there is no part of me that wishes to doubt the reality of the experience. Then, just behind me, to the right of my head, I sense the presence of Katrina, an old and very dear love who has recently given me a $3,000 loan with "when-you-can" repayment terms. Without her money, I would have been too broke to have the session. Then, another remarkable thing happens—Heather, my beloved, appears to me. I see her whole body enter and fill my emotional body, as though she is lying completely on top of me, but in the subtle realm. And, finally, I feel this extraordinary omnipotent beam of love from Allee, who is still massaging the knot.

I know that beautiful beings, human and otherwise, have come to this room especially for me. Carried to me on an inconceivable wave of love, they have come to help me heal. I feel the rock-hard cannonball start to stir. Suddenly, an explosion of emotion courses through me, and I begin to sob—deep, racking sobs, that continue in wave after wave for nearly an hour. Each time the sobbing stops, I feel the hardness of the block again, and then another wave of emotion bursts out of it, and I begin another bout of crying.

231

By the time the session ends, I have been with Allee nearly four hours. I realize this is not the norm, and that she has given me special attention. She brings me slowly back to the room, back to concrete reality, and she removes the beanbag from my eyes. I'm astonished to discover that it is still day. It feels as if it must be the middle of the night. I hold Allee's hand and tell her that she is the purest channel of love that I have ever known, and she says, "Oh, my ego loves to hear that!"

"I cannot imagine why your boyfriend," I say, "would ever let you go."

"Fear," she says. "Fear is all it is."

"He should do something about it."

"He's not ready," Allee replies.

Once I am dressed again, I say goodbye and give her a hug. "You're an angel," I tell her.

"That may be truer than you think," she replies with amusement. "I did come from the angelic realm and I have clear memories of it."

It takes the distance from her door to my car for the reply to sink in. Sitting on the tan vinyl seats of an aging, white Volvo station wagon, angelic realms seem impossibly remote, but at the same time entirely plausible—who, but a real angel, could have conducted such an exquisite symphony of healing?

The Miracle of Love is that it is both nothing and every-thing. It cannot be understood, and yet it is the source of all knowledge. It cannot be touched, and yet nothing exists without it.

Love holds the universe in perfect balance; it powers every living being; it brings life to all inanimate things; it creates all experience. It manifests in a speck of dust, in a blue whale calling across an ocean to its mate, in every cell, every star and throughout space. It is infinitely intelligent and benevolent. It can be trusted without question.

Love is who we are, and it is inconceivably vast. It is not compassion, though compassion is filled with it; neither is it caring, though caring is infused with its sweetness. Allowing, patience, growth, humor, healing, strength, guidance, gratitude, serenity, intuition, spirit, grace, intimacy—all of these are impelled by love, but love is far greater, far more encompassing, far more mysterious.

Love shines in the eyes of every sincere human being; it is an expression of our divinity. Though our love may be distorted by our wounds, and our actions become hurtful, everything we do is transmuted, by an alchemical miracle, into opportunities for healing. And so we should trust our love for one another; printed in a deeper reality than our conflicts, it is eternally present, working cease-lessly for our highest good.

233

ABOUT THE AUTHOR

JONATHAN COLLINS is the former Executive Director of the Ojai Institute, a study and retreat center that inquires into the fundamental nature of reality. He lives in Ojai, California, where he now devotes himself full time to writing.

For more information on the people featured in this book, please visit jonathancollins.com on the World Wide Web.